Needs of Male Sexual Assault Victims in the U.S. Armed Forces

Miriam Matthews, Coreen Farris, Margaret Tankard,
Michael Stephen Dunbar

T0308516

Prepared for the Office of the Secretary of Defense
Approved for public release; distribution unlimited

For more information on this publication, visit **www.rand.org/t/RR2167**

Library of Congress Cataloging-in-Publication Data is available for this publication.
ISBN: 978-1-9774-0031-4

Published by the RAND Corporation, Santa Monica, Calif.
© Copyright 2018 RAND Corporation
RAND® is a registered trademark.

Support RAND
Make a tax-deductible charitable contribution at
www.rand.org/giving/contribute

www.rand.org

Preface

Section 538 of the National Defense Authorization Act for Fiscal Year 2016 included a requirement to improve prevention of and response to sexual assaults in which the victim is a male member of the U.S. armed forces. To support this effort, RAND researchers reviewed previous research on male sexual assault and specifically considered research on male sexual assault in the U.S. armed forces. The researchers also conducted interviews with individuals who provide support services to U.S. military personnel and with civilian experts who study male sexual assault or provide services to victims. This report details the study's findings.

Although research considering the needs of and services for male sexual assault victims is more limited than research addressing female sexual assault victims, the available research provides initial information on the estimated prevalence, characteristics, consequences, and public perceptions of male sexual assault. This literature— along with the results of interviews that addressed needs of male sexual assault victims, reporting and help-seeking among victims, and knowledge and perceptions about such assaults—suggests potential avenues for better addressing the needs of male sexual assault victims in the U.S. armed forces. These avenues include improvements to reporting procedures, counseling services, outreach to victims, and education and training of service providers and servicemembers.

This research was sponsored by the Sexual Assault Prevention and Response Office in the Office of the Secretary of Defense and conducted within the Forces and Resources Policy Center of the RAND National Defense Research Institute, a federally funded research and development center sponsored by the Office of the Secretary of Defense, the Joint Staff, the Unified Combatant Commands, the Navy, the Marine Corps, the defense agencies, and the defense Intelligence Community.

For more information on the RAND Forces and Resources Policy Center, see www.rand.org/nsrd/ndri/centers/frp or contact the director (contact information is provided on the webpage).

Contents

Preface iii
Tables vii
Summary ix
Acknowledgments xxv
Abbreviations xxvii

CHAPTER ONE
Introduction 1
Review of the Literature 2
Interviews 3
Summary 7

CHAPTER TWO
Review of Previous Research on Male Sexual Assault Characteristics 9
Definition of Sexual Assault 9
Estimated Prevalence of Male Sexual Assault 10
Characteristics of Male Sexual Assault 11
Summary 19

CHAPTER THREE
Identifying and Addressing the Needs of Male Sexual Assault Victims 21
Perceived Needs of Victims 21
Meeting Male Victim Needs Through Provider Preparation 29
Summary 33

CHAPTER FOUR
Reporting and Help-Seeking Among Male Sexual Assault Victims 35
Likelihood of Reporting and Seeking Support 36
Gender Differences in Reporting and Help-Seeking 37
Amount of Time Victims Wait to Report 38
Predictors of Reporting and Help-Seeking 39

Barriers to Reporting and Help-Seeking... 40
Strategies to Improve Reporting and Help-Seeking 47
Summary... 50

CHAPTER FIVE
Improving Knowledge and Correcting Misperceptions About Male Sexual
    Assault 51
How Male Sexual Assault Victims Are Perceived 51
Perceptions of Campaigns to Educate Servicemembers About Male Sexual Assault 55
Interviewees' Suggestions on How to Improve Education Campaigns Addressing
    Male Sexual Assault... 58
Summary... 60

CHAPTER SIX
Recommendations 61

ONLINE APPENDIXES
Available for download at www.rand.org/t/RR2167
A. Military Service Provider Interview Protocol
B. Military Service Provider Code Case Counts, by Military Service and
    Area of Focus
C. Military Service Provider Code Case Counts, by Estimated Number of
    Victims Assisted

Bibliography 69

Tables

1.1. Topics Addressed in the Interview Protocol... 4
1.2. Number of Service Providers Interviewed, by Characteristic and Service Branch.. 6

Summary

In recent years, the public and Congress have shown increased interest in meeting the needs of male servicemembers who have been sexually assaulted (see, for example, Lamothe, 2015). In the National Defense Authorization Act for Fiscal Year (FY) 2016 (Pub. L. 114-92), Congress included a requirement to improve prevention of and response to sexual assaults against male members of the U.S. armed forces. In particular, Congress instructed the U.S. Department of Defense (DoD) to develop a plan to prevent and respond to sexual assaults of military men that specifically addresses the needs of male victims, including their medical and mental health care needs.[1] This report provides information relevant to this requirement. Specifically, the report contains information to assist with the implementation of DoD's *Plan to Prevent and Respond to Sexual Assault of Military Men* (DoD, 2016b).

To begin documenting the needs of male sexual assault victims in the U.S. military services, we first reviewed the published research on sexual assault against men, including the characteristics of perpetrators and victims, post-assault needs, associated services for male victims, and public perception of male victims. We then conducted semi-structured telephone interviews with eight experts external to DoD and 56 individuals who provide services to sexual assault victims in the U.S. military.[2] For this study, military service providers included chaplains, mental health care providers, physical health care providers (e.g., sexual assault nurse examiners, sexual assault medical forensic examiners), legal counsel (including special victims' counsel), special agents, sexual assault response coordinators, and victim advocates. Interview topics included needs, reporting, resources, and outreach related to male sexual assault vic-

---

[1] When we use the term *male sexual assault* in this report, we are referencing sexual assault against men. In addition, although individuals may alternatively be referred to as *survivors*, we use the term *victim* to reference individuals who have been sexually assaulted. There is not a clear consensus on which term should be used, and, when providing assistance to individuals, service providers recommend asking each individual which term he or she prefers (Rape, Abuse, and Incest National Network, 2016).

[2] This study was reviewed and approved by RAND's Human Subjects Protection Committee and DoD's Research Regulatory Oversight Office.

tims. The topics also included training for service providers and interviewees' work experiences involving public awareness of male sexual assault.[3]

Review of Previous Research on Male Sexual Assault Characteristics

Research addressing various aspects of male sexual assault, including estimated prevalence and characteristics, has slowly increased over the past several decades.

Definition of Sexual Assault

DoD Instruction 6495.02 defines *sexual assault*, similar to Article 120 of the Uniform Code of Military Justice (UCMJ) (10 U.S.C. 920), as

> intentional sexual contact characterized by the use of force, threats, intimidation, or abuse of authority or when the victim does not or cannot consent. As used in this Instruction, the term includes a broad category of sexual offenses consisting of the following specific UCMJ offenses: rape, sexual assault, aggravated sexual contact, abusive sexual contact, forcible sodomy (forced oral or anal sex), or attempts to commit these offenses. (DoD, 2013, p. 91)

To be clear, DoD defines *consent* to include "words or overt acts indicating a freely given agreement to the sexual conduct at issue by a competent person," and consent cannot be given if the person is "sleeping or incapacitated, such as due to age, alcohol or drugs, or mental incapacity" (DoD, 2012, p. 15). These definitions are consistent with most U.S. state statutes on sexual assault, the majority of which include both penetrative and nonpenetrative sexual contact crimes, offender behaviors beyond physical force (such as threats and intimidation), and situations in which the victim is not legally capable of providing consent (Tracy et al., 2012).

Prevalence of Male Sexual Assault

Although many researchers have estimated the prevalence of sexual assault against civilian men, these estimates have varied dramatically across studies (from 0.2 percent to 73 percent among community and university samples) (see Peterson et al., 2011, for a review). Part of the variation in reported estimates appears to be due to substantial sample variation, discrepancies in the time frames referenced across studies (e.g., lifetime, past 12 months), references to different behaviors or categories of behaviors, and other methodological variation across studies (Peterson et al., 2011). One survey that included men, the National Intimate Partner and Sexual Violence Survey (fielded in 2011), used 21 behaviorally specific items to measure rape, attempted rape, and other

---

[3] Review and analysis of all sexual assault prevention efforts administered across the services was outside the scope of the project.

sexual violence (Breiding et al., 2014). Based on this survey, the researchers estimated that 1.7 percent of men experienced an attempted or completed rape in their lifetime (compared with 19.3 percent of women). In addition, they estimated that 23.4 percent of men experienced other sexual violence in their lifetime (e.g., being made to penetrate someone else, sexual coercion, unwanted sexual contact).

Methodological and definitional differences across studies also appear to influence prevalence estimates among U.S. servicemen, and thus researchers have also reported a broad range of sexual assault rates for military men (from 0.02 percent to 12 percent) (Hoyt, Klosterman Rielage, and Williams, 2011). The most recent assessment of sexual assault against military men, the 2016 DoD Workplace and Gender Relations Survey of Active Duty Members (WGRA) (Davis et al., 2017), used methodology developed for the 2014 RAND Military Workplace Study (RMWS) (see Morral, Gore, and Schell, 2014). The 2014 RMWS was designed to address criticisms in prior research on military sexual assault. For example, the study relied on a large representative sample, obtained an acceptable survey response rate, and used behaviorally specific survey items that aligned with the sexual assault criteria outlined in Article 120 of the UCMJ (see Morral, Gore, and Schell, 2014). The 2016 fielding of the WGRA used these methods, and results showed that approximately 0.6 percent of active-duty men had experienced a sexual assault in the past year, with rates ranging from 0.3 percent in the Air Force to 0.9 percent in the Navy (Davis and Grifka, 2017a). For lifetime prevalence, the estimate was that 2.2 percent of active-duty men had experienced a sexual assault in their lifetime, and 1.8 percent had experienced a sexual assault since joining the military (Davis and Grifka, 2017a).

Characteristics of Male Sexual Assault

Beyond examining prevalence estimates, research has explored the characteristics of male sexual assault, including victim, perpetrator, and assault characteristics.

Perpetrator Characteristics

Among male servicemembers who had been sexually assaulted in the past year, 69 percent indicated that the perpetrator was a man or that the group of people who assaulted them included both men and women (Severance, Debus, and Davis, 2017). In addition, a substantial proportion of sexual assaults against active-duty servicemen involved more than one perpetrator (Severance, Debus, and Davis, 2017). Specifically, 33 percent of active-duty male sexual assault victims indicated that there were multiple offenders (Severance, Debus, and Davis, 2017). Among male servicemembers who were sexually assaulted in the past year, the largest proportion indicated that they were assaulted by a friend or acquaintance (43 percent), but many indicated that they were assaulted by a stranger (19 percent) or that they did not know who assaulted them (31 percent) (Severance, Debus, and Davis, 2017).

Among male civilians, 86 percent of those who reported the assault to civilian law enforcement indicated that the perpetrator was a man (Choudhary et al., 2012).

In addition, a larger proportion of civilian male sexual assaults than of civilian female sexual assaults appear to involve more than one perpetrator (Bullock and Beckson, 2011; McLean, 2013). Most perpetrators of sexual assault against civilian men also appear to be known to the victim (94 percent) (Choudhary et al., 2012).

Victim Characteristics

In terms of victim characteristics, servicemen who identified as gay, bisexual, or transgender were substantially more likely to be sexually assaulted in the past year (3.5 percent) than were those who did not identify as gay, bisexual, or transgender (0.3 percent) (Davis et al., 2017). Enlisted servicemen in lower pay grades were more likely than those in higher pay grades to be sexually assaulted (Severance, Debus, and Davis, 2017). Among active-duty servicemen who had experienced a sexual assault in the past year, most were under age 30 (71 percent), white (56 percent), and in junior enlisted pay grades (67 percent) (Severance, Debus, and Davis, 2017).

Research has shown that, among civilians, many (if not most) victims of male sexual assault are heterosexual (Bullock and Beckson, 2011; Isely and Gehrenbeck-Shim, 1997; McLean, 2013). However, gay or bisexual men experience sexual assault at higher rates than heterosexual men (Bullock and Beckson, 2011; Langenderfer-Magruder et al., 2016), and a 2009 study found that approximately 50 percent of transgender persons had experienced unwanted sexual activity in their lifetime (Stotzer, 2009). Research suggests that most civilian male victims in the United States are from a household with an income of either $25,000–$74,999 (50 percent) or less than $25,000 (46.4 percent) (Isely and Gehrenbeck-Shim, 1997; Weiss, 2010). In addition, most victims are non-Hispanic, white (Isely and Gehrenbeck-Shim, 1997; Weiss, 2010). Overall, both men and women with a history of childhood sexual abuse are at higher risk for experiencing sexual assault as an adult (Hines, 2007).

Assault Characteristics

In addition to examining the characteristics of perpetrators and victims of male sexual assault, studies have also examined the characteristics of the assaults perpetrated against male victims. Research has shown that, among servicemen who had been sexually assaulted in the past year, approximately one-third experienced a *penetrative* sexual assault (35 percent), and two-thirds experienced a *nonpenetrative* or *attempted penetrative* assault (65 percent) (Davis and Grifka, 2017a). The majority of sexual assaults perpetrated against civilian men involved penetrative anal assault (Bullock and Beckson, 2011; Hillman et al., 1991; Isely and Gehrenbeck-Shim, 1997; McLean, 2013; Stermac, del Bove, and Addison, 2004).

More than 40 percent of civilian male victims reported being assaulted in a residence (Choudhary et al., 2012; Isely and Gehrenbeck-Shim, 1997; Weiss, 2010). By contrast, a smaller proportion of military male victims reported being assaulted in a residence (25 percent) (Severance, Debus, and Davis, 2017). Most male, active-duty victims reported being sexually assaulted at a military installation or aboard a military ship (64 percent). Nearly half were assaulted at their workplace during duty hours (45 percent), and 31 percent were assaulted while out with friends or at a party (Severance, Debus, and Davis, 2017).

In addition to being sexually assaulted, approximately 30 percent to 40 percent of civilian male victims are physically injured, typically involving injuries to the perineal or anal area (McLean, 2013; Stermac, del Bove, and Addison, 2004), and 6 percent to 9 percent require medical attention (Stermac, del Bove, and Addison, 2004; Weiss, 2010). For military victims of male sexual assault, about one-half indicated that they were injured during the assault, but the type of injury was not assessed (Morral, Gore, and Schell, 2014). Assault-related injuries were more common among servicemen relative to servicewomen (Morral, Gore, and Schell, 2014).

An involuntary erection and ejaculation during sexual assault can occur for some male victims (Bullock and Beckson, 2011). For example, some men may experience an erection during times of intense fear or pain (Tewksbury, 2007). In addition, victims may intentionally ejaculate to minimize the assault duration, or offenders may make the victim ejaculate as a strategy to confuse the victim and discourage reporting (Fuchs, 2004). Research on arousal and ejaculation during a male sexual assault is limited, and no data are available on prevalence in a military sample. One study found that, among civilians, 18 percent of male victims who accessed sexual assault counseling services were stimulated to ejaculation (King and Woollett, 1997). Research reinforces that victim arousal or ejaculation is not indicative of victim consent (e.g., Bullock and Beckson, 2011; Fuchs, 2004).

Many sexual assaults against military men may be part of hazing acts. Drawing from the most recent reported estimates, military male victims (70 percent) were far more likely than military female victims (42 percent) to indicate that the assault was intended to abuse or humiliate them (Jaycox, Schell, Morral, et al., 2015). Other suggestions that military male sexual assault victims are more likely to be assaulted as part of hazing events than are military female victims include the fact that male victims (45 percent) are more likely than female victims (27 percent) to indicate that the assault took place at work during duty hours (Davis and Grifka, 2017b). Finally, military male victims (26 percent) are more than twice as likely as military female victims (10 percent) to label their worst sexual assault in the past year as a "hazing" incident (Severance, Debus, and Davis, 2017).

Identifying and Addressing the Needs of Male Sexual Assault Victims

To better address the needs of servicemen who have been sexually assaulted, it is necessary to first understand what those needs are and then ensure that service providers are appropriately trained to address the identified needs. We addressed these topics in our interviews.

Perceived Needs of Victims

Across the individuals we interviewed, the following were discussed as needs of all sexual assault victims and of male victims specifically: mental health care, advocacy, chain-of-command support, social support, information, legal support, and medical care. More interviewees discussed mental health care needs than any other need, and medical care needs were raised least often. The limited discussion of medical care needs among interviewees could be attributed to multiple factors, including delays in help-seeking until after physical symptoms have resolved and the limited number of physical health (e.g., medical) service providers in our sample.

When we asked interviewees to compare the needs of male and female sexual assault victims in the military, military service providers perceived that there were some differences between men and women. When discussing these differences, service providers tended to discuss gender differences in the barriers to accessing needed services rather than differences in the types of services needed. These barriers for men included concerns over stigma and reluctance to report.

Advocacy, Social Support, and Information

According to research with civilians, male sexual assault victims may isolate themselves from others, including emotionally distancing themselves and withdrawing from their social network (Walker, Archer, and Davies, 2005). Much of the research addressing military sexual assault among U.S. military veterans assesses a broad category of experiences that are labeled *military sexual trauma* (MST). MST, as defined by U.S. Department of Veterans Affairs screening questions, includes experiencing sexual contact via threat or force or experiencing unwanted sexual attention (e.g., touching, pressuring for sexual favors) while in the military (Maguen et al., 2012). Previous research showed that, among veterans who had been referred to a mental health clinic for anxiety, those who had experienced MST (1) perceived less support from those in their social network than those who had not experienced MST and (2) were more likely to indicate that they had been "shamed, embarrassed, or repeatedly told [they were] no good" (Mondragon et al., 2015).

To ensure that all military sexual assault victims have immediate access to advocacy, social support, and information, each service branch's Sexual Assault Prevention and Response or Sexual Harassment/Assault Response and Prevention program includes victim advocates who are available to guide victims through reporting decisions, provide information about available services, accompany victims to post-assault medical or legal appointments, address immediate safety needs, and offer support (DoD, 2013).

Support services may be particularly important to male victims. Four of the military service providers we interviewed believed that male sexual assault victims have less social support, and ten providers believed that male victims experience more shame than female victims. In addition, both previous research and comments from our interviewees suggest that male victims may need support to process concerns about sexual identity and perceived loss of masculinity that can arise after a sexual assault. Interviewee comments that emphasized male-specific concerns regarding sexuality and identity suggest that these might be areas where DoD should provide additional support.

Mental Health Care

According to the published literature on civilian sexual assaults, a large proportion of male sexual assault victims experience symptoms of depression, anxiety, nightmares, flashbacks, self-blame, low self-esteem, or problems with anger control following the assault (Isely and Gehrenbeck-Shim, 1997; Walker, Archer, and Davies, 2005). Among military veterans who sought care at a Department of Veterans Affairs facility, men and women who had experienced MST had higher odds of posttraumatic stress disorder (PTSD), other anxiety disorders, and depression than veterans who were not victims of MST during their military career (Kimerling et al., 2010; Maguen et al., 2012). Male victims, whether civilian or military, may experience suicidal ideation, and some may make a suicide attempt (Schry et al., 2015; Tiet, Finney, and Moos, 2006; Walker, Archer, and Davies, 2005). For male sexual assault victims who develop psychiatric conditions, such as major depressive disorder or PTSD, evidence-based treatments for these conditions are available. However, limited research has assessed the efficacy of mental health treatment specifically designed to assist male sexual assault victims.

Eighteen of the military service providers we interviewed believed that the military system could benefit from additional male-specific mental health services, such as men's support groups and counselors with greater knowledge of the needs of male sexual assault victims. Among the civilian experts we talked with, opinion was divided about the value of group-based therapy relative to individual therapy for male victims of sexual assault.

Career Support

The experience of MST among men serving in the military is strongly associated with military separation or retirement (Millegan et al., 2016). The military service providers we interviewed brought up the career support that victims may need, particularly support from their chain of command. The chain of command can support a victim's needs in a variety of ways, such as supporting access to services, which may require appointments during work hours. As one mental health care provider for the Air Force described,

> Primarily what [victims] are looking for from command is just support. So, allowing them to attend medical and mental health appointments as needed; reassignment if that's something that they desire or something that everyone agrees would be in the victim's best interest. And so, primarily [they need] support.

Medical Care

Our interviews with civilian and military experts did not often address the medical care needs of victims. One civilian researcher noted that research shows that male victims experience more-violent assaults with greater risk of injury and added that this will affect "what sort of injuries and what sort of mental and physical trauma needs to be attended to."

Other Needs

Interviewees noted that male victims may also have legal, spiritual, or financial needs following an assault, but these needs were not discussed in as much detail as those previously described. In addition, military service providers specifically commented on victims' concerns about privacy, which we discuss more later.

Meeting Male Victim Needs Through Provider Preparation

Male victims often seek help for a variety of individualized needs, ranging from short-term advocacy and medical care to longer-term mental health support. Military service providers working in the sexual assault, medical, mental health, chaplaincy, and legal fields may already have training to support female victims that can be readily translated to care for male victims. In other cases, additional training in addressing the unique needs of male victims or in ensuring a sensitive, gender-specific approach toward men may be necessary.

Researchers recommend that the curriculum used to train military service providers include factual information about male sexual assault and address common myths about sexual assault against men and women (Anderson and Quinn, 2009; Kassing and Prieto, 2003). If service providers build a factual foundation of information about male sexual assault and understand the potential impact of false beliefs on male victims, they will be in a better position to counter the harmful false narratives that victims may believe about themselves (e.g., "I should have been able to stop it") and that others might believe about them (Davies, 2002). Researchers have also recommended ways that service providers should interact with male sexual assault victims. For example, researchers recommend establishing good rapport when a victim initially comes forward and suggest using normalizing statements, such as "Everyone takes time to deal with an assault" (Tomlinson and Harrison, 1998, p. 721).

Among the military service providers we spoke to about service provider preparation, most believed that individuals in their profession were either somewhat informed or well informed about sexual assault against men in the military.[4] However, this was not consistent across all professions. Specifically, only two chaplains believed that those in the chaplaincy were somewhat informed or well informed about assisting male vic-

---

[4] When we summarize interviewee comments, the terms *most* and *majority* indicate that more than half of those who commented on a specific topic or responded to a particular question provided comments that were coded as the referenced theme.

tims. In response to being asked how well prepared military chaplains were to serve male victims, an Army chaplain stated, "I think I could sell it very short and say not very. And I think that's true from a models standpoint. We're not taught any models anywhere in the Army for modalities for treating survivors of sexual assault."

Among military service providers who discussed the extent to which their training addressed male sexual assault, interviewees provided mixed responses. Almost half of those who responded recalled that their training provided either some information or a great deal of information on male sexual assault. However, slightly more than half of those who responded recalled that their training provided little or no such information. Most service providers who addressed training needs believed that more training on male sexual assault would be helpful.

Reporting and Help-Seeking Among Male Sexual Assault Victims

Following a sexual assault, victims make a series of decisions about whether to disclose the assault and to whom. They may choose to reach out to informal support persons, such as friends and family, or they may want or need assistance from formal support persons, such as sexual assault advocates, health care providers, and mental health counselors. Some victims may choose to involve the criminal justice system by reporting the crime or applying for a restraining order against the perpetrator. For civilians, each of these decisions can be made relatively independently. For military members, this is also true, with the exception that involving the military criminal justice system requires also involving the chain of command. U.S. military personnel who experience a sexual assault and choose to report it officially may file either a restricted or an unrestricted report. A *restricted report* is a confidential report that allows victims to access advocate support and medical and mental health care. Filing an *unrestricted report* allows the victim to access all the same services that a restricted report allows; in addition, filing an unrestricted report begins a criminal investigation, and the sexual assault report is disclosed to the victim's chain of command.

Likelihood of Reporting and Seeking Support

Estimates suggest that only 15 percent of military male sexual assault victims file a report (Severance, Debus, and Davis, 2017). Data published in 2017 show that, of victims who did report, 31 percent filed a restricted report, 55 percent filed an unrestricted report, and 15 percent were not sure what type of report they filed (Severance, Debus, and Davis, 2017). These findings are consistent with reporting among civilians. Although civilians can report to law enforcement without their employer being notified, the majority of civilian male sexual assault victims choose not to involve the criminal justice system (Pino and Meier, 1999).

Although victims who sought the services of our interviewees were, by definition, receptive to their services, the military service providers we spoke with described some variability in the degree to which victims were willing to seek care from other service providers. It was common for the military service providers we spoke with to indicate that they often provide referrals for services outside their specialty area.

Five out of the seven civilian experts who commented on this topic noted that male victims' reluctance to report or access services is a key challenge to connecting them to resources. Several indicated that, even among individuals seeking treatment for sexual assault–related conditions, there may be distrust of this treatment or of other suggested resources.

Gender Differences in Reporting and Help-Seeking

Servicewomen who experience a sexual assault are significantly more likely to file a report (31 percent) than are servicemen (15 percent) (Severance, Debus, and Davis, 2017). Both the civilian experts and military service providers we spoke with perceived that reporting was less common among men who had been sexually assaulted relative to women, and men may be less receptive than women to following up with resources.

Amount of Time Victims Wait to Report

When queried, most of the civilian experts we spoke with (six out of seven who responded) indicated that there is a wide range or too much variability across individuals to provide a reasonable estimate on gender differences in the amount of time individuals wait to report. Most military service providers who made a comparison did not perceive a gender difference in time to report among the male and female victims. They did, however, note that victims may wait to report until they are in a location that is away from their perpetrator. When commenting on trends in male sexual assault reporting, one provider responsible for sexual assault response in the Air Force said, "Instead of being on site or on station where the individual [perpetrator] was," the victim "waited until they went [on temporary duty] or deployed and then reported because they weren't where the individual was."

Predictors of Reporting and Help-Seeking

Greater severity of sexual assault appears to be associated with greater odds that male victims will seek help. Specifically, male victims are more likely to seek help when the perpetrator used threats during the incident and the victim believed he was at risk of being physically injured (Masho and Alvanzo, 2009). Among servicemen who experienced a sexual assault in the past year and who chose to report it, the most common motivations for reporting were to stop the offender from hurting others (45 percent) or themselves again (47 percent) (Severance, Debus, and Davis, 2017), or because they believed it was their civil or military duty to report (41 percent) (Severance, Debus, and Davis, 2017).

The military service providers we interviewed discussed several motivating factors for victims' reporting, including a desire to obtain justice, to prevent or stop an assault from happening to others, and to access certain rights or services. The providers also mentioned encouragement from others to report the assault; the assault having negative effects on the victim's life (e.g., intimate relationships); and, for some, unintentional reporting as a consequence of discussing the assault with a mandated reporter (e.g., a commander) or colleagues. Of these, the largest number of providers discussed the victim's desire to access rights or services as a motivator for reporting.

Barriers to Reporting and Help-Seeking

There are several reasons that some sexual assault victims choose not to report an assault or not to seek services or support following an assault. In some cases, the victim may not be personally aware of the barriers. For example, victims who do not label the incident as a sexual assault may not be aware that this is preventing them from accessing services that could help them. In other cases, the decision whether to report is based on the victim's calculus about likely outcomes. If sexual assault victims believe that their report will not be believed or acted upon; that they will be shamed, harmed, or retaliated against for reporting; or that the system cannot protect their confidentiality, many will decide that not disclosing will protect their interests better than reporting would. Notably, servicemen who indicate being penetrated or touched on their private areas during a hazing assault are unlikely to categorize the event as "sex."[5] Because their perpetrator(s) may not have been sexually aroused during the incident, the victims might not classify what happened to them as "sexual assault."

In addition, servicemen may lack confidence in the military system and, therefore, may not report. The military service providers we interviewed commented on this lack of confidence in the system and the common fear among male victims that they will not be believed even if they do come forward. One Navy mental health care provider noted,

> For men, I don't think they even think they'll be believed . . . . If they're gay, they think that, "oh, everyone is going to think it was consensual." And then if they're straight, then they think, "oh, everyone is going to think that really I'm gay, and I really wanted it." . . . Whether they're gay or straight, it doesn't seem to matter. They both feel like they're somehow going to be judged to be participants in it and willing participants in it.

Many sexual assault victims also choose not to report their assault or not to seek advocacy, medical care, or mental health care services because they believe that there will be negative consequences for doing so. Military service providers mentioned victim concerns about possible disciplinary actions for collateral misconduct (e.g., underage drinking prior to the assault) and emphasized worry about the impact of reporting on military careers.

---

[5] *Private areas* typically include buttocks, inner thigh, breasts, groin, anus, vagina, penis, or testicles.

Among U.S. servicemen, stereotypes about masculinity, including views of men as sexually assertive and powerful, and men's beliefs in male sexual assault myths may hinder reporting and help-seeking among victims (Castro et al., 2015; Morris et al., 2014). The military service providers we interviewed noted that military victims' self-blame, embarrassment, and shame are significant barriers to reporting and connecting them to services, and the providers identified embarrassment as a particularly potent barrier for male victims.

Further, evidence suggests that barriers to reporting and help-seeking, for both veterans and active-duty servicemembers, include the desire to maintain one's privacy and a lack of confidence in the confidentiality of medical, mental health, or other services (Turchik, McLean, et al., 2013). Privacy concerns were cited as a common barrier to reporting and help-seeking by the military service providers we interviewed.

Finally, some researchers have proposed that low rates of male sexual assault reporting in the U.S. military may be related to a perceived code of silence regarding these experiences and concern that reporting may be seen as betraying one's unit, particularly if the perpetrator or perpetrators are part of the unit (Castro et al., 2015). It is also notable that sexual assault is one of the few events that is exempt from military guidance to resolve conflict "at the lowest possible level." For example, even service members who are sexually harassed are encouraged to resolve the conflict directly or as low in their own military chain of command as possible. In a culture that trains individuals to prioritize direct conflict resolution, it may be psychologically difficult for male sexual assault victims to elevate their complaint even though they are allowed by policy to do so.

Strategies to Improve Reporting and Help-Seeking

One avenue for promoting help-seeking among male servicemembers who have experienced sexual assault is to dispel myths that those in the U.S. military community may believe regarding male sexual assault. To do so, researchers suggest including examples of male sexual assault survivors in educational materials (O'Brien, Keith, and Shoemaker, 2015). These materials should also include accurate information about sexual assault against men and women to counteract the inaccurate myths that some servicemembers may believe (Turchik and Edwards, 2012).

In addition, if the military provides training and educational materials that include male sexual assault victims, male servicemembers who experience sexual assault may not only be more willing to seek help following an assault but may also be more willing to report their assault through official channels (O'Brien, Keith, and Shoemaker, 2015; Scarce, 1997; Turchik and Edwards, 2012). However, if victims perceive that those to whom they report will react negatively or with disbelief, they may be unlikely to report being sexually assaulted. To promote reporting, male sexual assault victims must know that the professionals to whom they disclose will not express negative attitudes toward them or disbelief in their account of the assault (Javaid, 2017).

Improving Knowledge and Correcting Misperceptions About Male Sexual Assault Victims

Much of the research on male sexual assault has specifically considered public perceptions of such assault, including false and prejudicial beliefs, and the potential impact of these perceptions on male victims (Davies and Rogers, 2006; Light and Monk-Turner, 2009).

How Male Sexual Assault Victims Are Perceived

As suggested previously, among all military sexual assault victims, approximately half are men (Morral, Gore, and Schell, 2015b). Nonetheless, male sexual assault victims continue to be underrecognized and underserved for a variety of reasons (Castro et al., 2015; Turchik and Edwards, 2012). During our interviews, we asked civilian experts and military service providers their thoughts about how the general population and general military population perceived male victims of sexual assault.

Among military service providers, opinions were mixed about whether the general military population had an adequate understanding that men can be victims of sexual assault. Although male sexual assault is addressed in military sexual assault prevention training, some military providers believed that servicemembers maintain their stereotypes regarding male sexual assault even after receiving this training. In our discussions with research experts on civilian sexual assault, all of the experts who offered a comparison of the general public's understanding of male sexual assault (six) agreed that the public has greater knowledge or understanding of sexual assaults against women than of those perpetrated against men.

Reduced reporting among men, as well as limited public understanding, may keep the population of male victims more hidden than the population of female victims. The lack of public exposure to men who have survived a sexual assault may explain, in part, some individuals' acceptance of myths about sexual assault against men. *Sexual assault myths*, also known as *rape myths*, include false beliefs about sexual assault and beliefs that hold victims responsible for the assault while justifying the actions of the perpetrators (Chapleau, Oswald, and Russell, 2008).

Perceptions of Campaigns to Educate Servicemembers About Male Sexual Assault

Given evidence that servicemembers may not recognize that male sexual assault can occur and may have other misconceptions about such assaults, it seems clear that efforts to improve this population's understanding are needed. In the published literature, researchers have advocated for education that would dispel myths about sexual assault against both men and women (Turchik and Edwards, 2012) and have encouraged inclusion of examples of male sexual assault survivors in educational materials (O'Brien, Keith, and Shoemaker, 2015). The U.S. military services provide annual sexual assault prevention and response training to all servicemembers (see, for example, DoD, 2013), and it appears to increase knowledge of available support services and protocols (Holland, Rabelo, and Cortina, 2014).

In our interviews, we queried the perceived efficacy of outreach efforts. Most service providers who responded to this question indicated that they believed that the outreach campaigns were effective. The providers often noted that they believed that the campaigns had promoted sexual assault awareness or sexual assault reporting in the military population. However, opinions about the efficacy of efforts were not universal. Ten interviewees indicated that they perceived the campaigns as only somewhat effective, and eight noted that they were not certain how effective the campaigns were.

Interviewees' Suggestions on How to Improve Education Campaigns Addressing Male Sexual Assault

The civilian experts we interviewed provided a range of recommendations for improving sexual assault outreach campaigns. Two out of the six civilian experts who commented on this topic noted that there are lessons to be learned from successful safety and public health campaigns that have shifted societal norms. Discussing the recommendations that messaging address myths about male victims and that research support is necessary, one interviewee described the potential value of aligning conceptions of masculinity with the courage required to come forward as a survivor.

With respect to educating the military public about male sexual assault in particular, military service providers suggested, among other options, providing servicemembers with specific information about the characteristics of male sexual assaults and developing outreach materials that specifically address such assaults.

Recommendations

Information from previous research and our interviews with experts and military service providers suggest several potential avenues for DoD to consider as part of its efforts to improve prevention and response to sexual assaults against male victims. In this section, we provide several recommendations that draw from this previous research and our interviews.

Better educate military service providers on how to provide gender-responsive support to male sexual assault victims.

Previous research and interview results suggest that military service providers who might interact with male sexual assault victims should receive training on how to assist these individuals. This training should inform service providers of the concerns and needs of male victims, including feelings of shame, feelings of self-blame, confusion regarding sexual identity, perceived loss of masculinity, and concerns over privacy. Training should also provide a grounding in the common experiences of male victims and the variance in male victim thoughts and actions following an assault, as well as information that counters commonly held male sexual assault myths. In addition, the training should include practice and role-play. This would give service providers some practice talking about the topic and the opportunity to receive feedback from a trainer about areas of strength and areas requiring additional practice.

Promote male victim reporting by ensuring that reporting is safe and confidential.

An issue raised in previous research and during our interviews with experts and service providers is that the majority of male sexual assault victims are disinclined to report. In the military, this can include a disinclination to file restricted or unrestricted reports. These reports are connected to the availability of a variety of services for victims. However, reporting is also perceived to be related to a considerable risk of social or professional retaliation (Morral, Gore, and Schell, 2015b) and potential harm to the individual's career. In other words, victims make an individual calculus that weighs the benefits of reporting against the risks, and many decide that the risks are too considerable and the benefits too limited. Therefore, improving reporting rates will need to be a two-pronged approach. First, the reporting system must be improved to ensure that reassurances that reporting will not lead to retaliation or career harm are true. Second, male victims should be encouraged to report. As discussed later, training and education might assist servicemembers with identifying sexual assault and may promote reporting.

Change outreach to better address the needs and concerns of male sexual assault victims.

Additional outreach campaigns that are targeted specifically to male sexual assault victims, rather than those that are gender-neutral or targeted to female victims, might better promote male victim reporting and help-seeking, as suggested by several experts and service providers. Male victims who feel shame, perceive stigma, and experience doubts about their masculinity may find it challenging to absorb the information from a brochure or poster that primarily depicts women. In addition, reaching out to a sexual assault response coordinator or mental health care provider appears to be too high a hurdle for many male victims. To address this barrier, campaigns for men could emphasize services that do not require in-person appointments.

When educating servicemembers on sexual assault prevention and response, use an engaging format that includes information on the characteristics of male sexual assault.

Based on the information provided by our interviewees, it is not clear whether additional sexual assault prevention and response training sessions that address only male sexual assault are needed. However, substantial portions of the training and education provided to servicemembers should specifically address male sexual assault. In particular, training and education should include detailed information regarding the characteristics of male sexual assault among servicemembers, which may reference the occurrence of sexual assault during acts of hazing. To dispel common myths, education and training should focus on providing and reinforcing accurate information about the characteristics and experiences of victims.

Educate commanders on how to respond to male sexual assault and how to interact with male victims.

To better address the needs of male sexual assault victims and their concerns regarding stigma, commanders should receive training that specifically addresses the sexual assault of male servicemembers. This training content should include common characteristics of male sexual assault in the military, needs and concerns of male sexual assault victims, and appropriate and inappropriate ways to interact with and assist these victims. This training should also emphasize the importance of maintaining victim privacy and confidentiality.

Consider development and evaluation of additional counseling services that address the mental health care needs of male sexual assault victims in the military.

Service providers we interviewed suggested that DoD could devote more resources to the development and implementation of counseling resources for male sexual assault victims in the military. Potential counseling services that DoD could consider developing, implementing, and evaluating include small, structured support groups with male sexual assault victims in the military; increased use of online support groups or telephone-based support groups for such victims; and longer available duty hours of installation clinics.

Support additional research that addresses the effects of training, outreach, and services addressing male sexual assault.

When implementing a new effort or modifying a current effort to better address male sexual assault in the U.S. armed forces, DoD should devote time and resources to evaluating the impact and efficacy of these efforts. Overall, systematic data collection and analysis can provide information about which elements are effective and which elements may need to be modified to better address the needs of servicemembers broadly and male sexual assault victims specifically.

Acknowledgments

The authors wish to thank Nate Galbreath, deputy director of the U.S. Department of Defense Sexual Assault Prevention and Response Office (SAPRO); Bette Inch, senior victim assistance adviser for SAPRO; CAPT Karmon Dyches; Stephen Axelrad; and Jim Hopper for their assistance with this project. We would also like to thank the experts and military service providers who participated in discussions with us. In addition, we thank Andrew Morral, Terry Schell, John Winkler, Craig Bond, Kristie Gore, Lisa Harrington, and Sarah Meadows for their guidance and feedback throughout this project. We also thank Rajeev Ramchand and Rachel Kimerling for their thorough reviews and helpful comments on drafts of this report.

Abbreviations

DoD	U.S. Department of Defense
FY	fiscal year
MST	military sexual trauma
NCVS	National Crime Victimization Survey
NIBRS	National Incident-Based Reporting System
PTSD	posttraumatic stress disorder
RMWS	RAND Military Workplace Study
SAPR	sexual assault prevention and response
SAPRO	Sexual Assault Prevention and Response Office
SARC	sexual assault response coordinator
UCMJ	Uniform Code of Military Justice
VA	U.S. Department of Veterans Affairs
WGRA	Workplace and Gender Relations Survey of Active Duty Members

CHAPTER ONE

Introduction

Each year, an estimated 0.6 percent of active-duty men and 4.3 percent of active-duty women in the U.S. military are sexually assaulted (Davis and Grifka, 2017a). Although women are at greater risk for sexual assault, men substantially outnumber women in the military; therefore, about half of all military sexual assault victims are men (Morral, Gore, and Schell, 2015b). Relative to research addressing the characteristics and consequences of sexual assault against women and the subsequent needs of female sexual assault victims, less research has been conducted on male sexual assault, particularly sexual assault against men serving in the U.S. military.[1]

In recent years, the public and Congress have shown increased interest in meeting the needs of male servicemembers who have been sexually assaulted (see, for example, Lamothe, 2015). In the National Defense Authorization Act for Fiscal Year (FY) 2016 (Pub. L. 114-92), Congress included a requirement to improve prevention of and response to sexual assaults against male members of the U.S. armed forces. In particular, Congress instructed the U.S. Department of Defense (DoD) to develop a plan to prevent and respond to sexual assaults of servicemen that specifically addresses the needs of male victims, including their medical and mental health care needs. The resulting DoD *Plan to Prevent and Respond to Sexual Assault of Military Men* (DoD, 2016b, p. 3) documents that

> the Department is now working to increase research-informed, gender-specific prevention techniques that address male specific approaches to increase awareness of male sexual assault, ensure response services meet the specific needs of male survivors, and promote male engagement with the response system.

The research conducted for this report responds, in part, to a Sexual Assault Prevention and Response Office (SAPRO) plan to "identify new research efforts in

---

[1] When we use the term *male sexual assault* in this report, we are referencing sexual assault against men. In addition, although individuals may alternatively be referred to as *survivors*, we use the term *victim* to reference individuals who have been sexually assaulted. There is not a clear consensus on which term should be used, and when providing assistance to individuals, service providers recommend asking each individual which term he or she prefers (Rape, Abuse, and Incest National Network, 2016).

order to better understand the experiences and needs of male survivors" (DoD, 2016b, p. 4). Specifically, this report contains information to assist with the implementation of DoD's *Plan to Prevent and Respond to Sexual Assault of Military Men*. It documents military service providers' and non-DoD experts' opinions about the needs of male sexual assault victims in the U.S. military and includes recommendations about how the needs of these victims could be addressed through education, outreach, training, and response systems.[2]

Review of the Literature

To begin documenting the needs of male sexual assault victims in the U.S. military, we first reviewed the published research on sexual assault against men, including the characteristics of perpetrators and victims, post-assault needs, associated services for male victims, and public perception of male victims. Although we considered some research on child sexual abuse, we focused on studies of adult men. We considered research on

- sexual assault against all men
- sexual assault against U.S. military servicemen, including current active-duty personnel, reserve personnel (National Guard and Reserve), and veterans
- services for male sexual assault victims
- public perception of male sexual assault victims.

We used the Google Scholar database to search the Online Computer Library Center's WorldCat (undated) and research databases available via the RAND Corporation's Knowledge Services, including LexisNexis, EBSCO, and ProQuest, among others. We searched English-language literature, including research focused on populations outside of the United States, that had been published since January 2005, using relevant keywords and phrases. Example search terms included "male sexual assault," "male rape," "male sexual trauma," "male victims" AND "sexual assault," "male victims" AND "rape," "male victims" AND "sexual trauma," and ("male" OR "men") AND "military sexual trauma." After establishing a preliminary list of relevant studies, we reviewed the references listed in the studies to identify additional research. We also asked informed colleagues to review this list and identify research that had been overlooked. Our final list included 98 sources.

---

[2]   Review and analysis of all sexual assault prevention efforts administered across the services was outside the scope of the project.

Interviews

To gain insight into the needs of male sexual assault victims, we conducted semi-structured telephone interviews with eight experts external to DoD and 56 individuals who provide services to sexual assault victims in the U.S. military (hereafter referred to as *military service providers*).[3] For this study, military service providers included chaplains, mental health care providers, physical health care providers (e.g., sexual assault nurse examiners, sexual assault medical forensic examiners), legal counsel (including special victims' counsel), special agents, sexual assault response coordinators (SARCs), and victim advocates. Interview topics included needs, reporting, resources, and outreach related to male sexual assault victims. The topics also included training for service providers and interviewees' work experiences involving public awareness of male sexual assault. The eight experts external to DoD discussed the topics broadly, without a specific focus on military personnel, and military service providers discussed the topics with a specific focus on U.S. military personnel.

Materials

We developed the interview protocols based on our literature review and the topics raised in Section 538 of the FY 2016 National Defense Authorization Act. Representatives from SAPRO and one expert outside DoD provided feedback on the protocols. Ultimately, the interview protocols contained eight sections. One of the sections assessed the characteristics and professional experience of the interviewee, and the concluding section gathered general comments and recommendations. The remaining six sections addressed specific areas related to male sexual assault (Table 1.1). Within each section, the protocol included queries addressing sexual assault victims in general and male sexual assault victims specifically or comparisons between male and female sexual assault victims. For the complete interview protocol, see Appendix A of this report, available for download at www.rand.org/t/RR2167. Appendixes B and C (also available online) provide tables listing the number and type of military service providers who commented on each theme (e.g., the amount of time that had elapsed between an assault and the victim reporting the assault, victims' need for legal counsel support) during the interviews.

---

[3] This study was reviewed and approved by RAND's Human Subjects Protection Committee and DoD's Research Regulatory Oversight Office.

Table 1.1
Topics Addressed in the Interview Protocol

Topic	Sample Question
Interviewee characteristics	How many, if any, male sexual assault victims have you assisted?
Needs	What are the needs male servicemember sexual assault victims, in particular, may have?
Reporting	What are the most common reasons servicemembers who are sexual assault victims do NOT report the assault?
Resources	What are the most common resources you offer to a victim of military sexual assault?
Knowledge and perceptions of victims	What do servicemembers know about the sexual assault of male servicemembers?
Outreach	Are you aware of any current outreach campaigns to prevent and respond to military sexual assault?
Training	In your experience, how informed are [respondent's professional group] about male sexual assault in the military?
Parting observations and recommendations	Do you have any additional suggestions about how DoD could better serve male sexual assault victims?

Recruitment and Sample Description

To create each sample of interviewees, we used a purposeful, or nonprobability, approach (Patton, 2015). For the expert interviews, we invited those employed by or affiliated with organizations that focus on providing services to male sexual assault victims and researchers who had published peer-reviewed articles on male sexual assault. We obtained their contact information from the articles they had published or their employer's website. The final sample consisted of four mental health care providers, one physical health care provider, and three researchers.

For the military service provider sample, we first identified three installations for each service branch where providers would be more likely to have worked with male sexual assault victims than providers serving at other installations. The three installations included locations where men might be at a higher risk of sexual assault relative to other installations in the same military service. We identified these installations using analyses of the RAND Military Workplace Study (RMWS) (for more information on this survey and data, see Morral, Gore, and Schell, 2014, and especially Morral et al., forthcoming).[4] We then modified our initial list of installations based on feedback

---

[4]   Notably, DoD's 2016 Workplace and Gender Relations Survey of Active Duty Members (WGRA) draws from the methods of the 2014 RMWS, which we discuss in Chapter Two.

from service representatives. For example, an alternative installation was requested because a selected installation was already participating in research requiring service provider time. The installations included in the interview sample were as follows:

- Army
  - Fort Bragg
  - Fort Campbell
  - Fort Hood
- Navy
  - Naval Base San Diego
  - Naval Station Great Lakes
  - Naval Station Norfolk
- Air Force
  - Hurlburt Field Air Force Base
  - Lackland Air Force Base
  - Minot Air Force Base
- Marine Corps
  - Marine Corps Air Station Cherry Point
  - Marine Corps Air Ground Combat Center 29 Palms
  - Marine Corps Base Camp Pendleton.

For each selected installation, service representatives provided us with contact information for at least one chaplain, mental health care provider, physical health care provider, legal counsel, and SARC or victim advocate who was likely to have worked with male sexual assault victims. Individuals from our research team emailed providers an invitation to participate in a research interview, which included information about the RAND Corporation and this study. The invitation email included the study's informed consent document as an attachment and requested a one-hour phone conversation on a date and time convenient for the service provider. We sent a subsequent email one week after the initial email to individuals who had not yet responded. One week after this reminder email, we called individuals who had not yet responded.

In addition to the eight experts external to DoD, 15 providers affiliated with the Army, 17 with the Navy, 12 with the Air Force, and 12 with the Marine Corps participated in an interview. Table 1.2 summarizes service provider characteristics, including the number of male sexual assault victims they had assisted.[5]

---

[5]   We also asked service providers whether they had assisted friends, family, spouses, or partners of male sexual assault victims. However, very few service providers indicated that they had provided services to these individuals, so we do not include such information in this report.

Table 1.2
Number of Service Providers Interviewed, by Characteristic and Service Branch

Characteristic	Service Branch			
	Army	Navy	Air Force	Marine Corps
Gender				
Male	7	9	5	7
Female	8	8	5	5
Gender not provided	0	0	2	0
Military experience				
Active-duty servicemember	10	8	9	7
Veteran	4	3	2	2
Neither active duty nor veteran	1	6	1	3
Area of focus				
Chaplain	3	3	2	2
Mental or behavioral health care	2	5	2	3
Physical health care	2	3	2	2
Legal counsel[a]	3	3	3	3
Sexual assault response[b]	5	3	3	2
Interviewee-estimated number of all (male and female) sexual assault victims assisted during career[c]				
None	0	0	0	0
1 to 12	3	0	1	0
13 to 24	2	4	3	0
25 or more	9	12	8	9
Estimate not available	1	1	0	3
Interviewee-estimated number of male sexual assault victims assisted during career[c]				
None	2	0	0	0
1 to 12	11	9	12	8
13 to 24	1	3	0	1
25 or more	1	4	0	3
Estimate not available	0	1	0	0

[a] Includes victims' legal counsel, special victims' counsel, and judge advocates.

[b] Includes SARCs, victim advocates, and special agents.

[c] When interviewees provided a range, we used the midpoint to categorize them. For example, someone who had assisted "20 to 30 victims" would be categorized as assisting 25. When interviewees indicated that they had assisted more than a certain number, we used one number above the number provided to categorize them. For example, someone who had assisted "more than 12 victims" would be categorized as assisting 13. Those who did not provide a number or range (e.g., "quite a few," "not many") were categorized as not having an available estimate.

Interview and Data Analysis Procedures

Four RAND researchers conducted one-on-one, semi-structured telephone interviews with participants between February and April 2017. After obtaining consent from each participant, the interviewers audio-recorded each interview. All interviews were then transcribed verbatim. We uploaded all transcripts to Dedoose, a research tool for qualitative and mixed-methods data analysis (Dedoose, 2017), and used a two-stage process to code the interviews. In the first stage, we developed a preliminary codebook that corresponded to the specific questions in the interview protocol (see Appendix A). In the second stage, two RAND researchers coded the interviews. We developed subcodes within each question based on transcript themes that arose from interviewee comments, which we discussed in weekly meetings. We tested code application agreement using the Dedoose training module, focusing on code reliability within protocol sections. The pooled Cohen's kappa statistic was 0.97, which demonstrates good reliability (Bernard and Ryan, 2010).

Because of the small sample size and variation in expert background, we did not expect the number or proportion of interviewees who provided comments relevant to each theme to be a meaningful reflection of the prevalence of different expert viewpoints. Given that the sample size was too small for generalization or subgroup analysis, in the chapters that follow, we focus instead on describing the themes that arose and using illustrative quotes to complement these descriptions. As noted previously, Appendixes B and C contain tables of the number and type of interviewee who commented on each theme.

Summary

This chapter provided the policy context that motivated the research presented in this report and described the research study. Methods included a review of the published literature, semi-structured interviews with non-DoD experts on male sexual assault, and semi-structured interviews with military service providers. The interview protocol included sections focused on male sexual assault victims' needs, reporting decisions, and resources; provider perception of the general population's knowledge and attitudes toward male sexual assault victims; and provider knowledge and perception of outreach activities and their own training. About half of the service providers in the sample were women, and interviewee experience ranged from not having worked directly with a male sexual assault victim to having worked with hundreds of male victims in group therapy.

CHAPTER TWO

Review of Previous Research on Male Sexual Assault Characteristics

In this chapter, we introduce the DoD definition of sexual assault; review estimates of the prevalence of sexual assault against men; and review previous research that has considered perpetrator, victim, and assault characteristics. Throughout, we review research assessing community and nonmilitary samples, as well as research specifically addressing the U.S. military, including current active-duty personnel, reserve personnel (National Guard and Reserve), and veterans.

Definition of Sexual Assault

DoD Instruction 6495.02 defines *sexual assault*, similar to Article 120 of the Uniform Code of Military Justice (UCMJ) (10 U.S.C. 920), as

> intentional sexual contact characterized by the use of force, threats, intimidation, or abuse of authority or when the victim does not or cannot consent. As used in this Instruction, the term includes a broad category of sexual offenses consisting of the following specific UCMJ offenses: rape, sexual assault, aggravated sexual contact, abusive sexual contact, forcible sodomy (forced oral or anal sex), or attempts to commit these offenses. (DoD, 2013, p. 91)

To be clear, DoD defines consent to include "words or overt acts indicating a freely given agreement to the sexual conduct at issue by a competent person," and consent cannot be satisfied if the person is "sleeping or incapacitated, such as due to age, alcohol or drugs, or mental incapacity" (DoD, 2012, p. 15). These definitions are consistent with most U.S. state statutes on sexual assault, the majority of which include both penetrative and nonpenetrative sexual contact crimes, offender behaviors beyond physical force (such as threats and intimidation), and situations in which the victim is not legally capable of providing consent (Tracy et al., 2012).

Until recently, many laws in the United States did not recognize the possibility of male victims of sexual assault. U.S. law has typically, and often explicitly, viewed rape as specific to female victims (Fuchs, 2004). Until 2012, assaults against men were also largely excluded from Article 120 definitions of rape and sexual assault, both of which limited "sexual acts" to contact between the penis and vulva or penetration of the genital opening. The 2012 revisions to Article 120 expanded the definitions of rape and sexual assault to apply to male victims by updating them to include sexual acts that men can experience (i.e., contact between the penis and the vulva, anus, or mouth; or penetration of the vulva, anus, or mouth) (10 U.S.C. 920).

Estimated Prevalence of Male Sexual Assault

Although many researchers have estimated the prevalence of sexual assault against civilian men, these estimates have varied dramatically across studies (from 0.2 percent to 73 percent among community and university samples) (see Peterson et al., 2011, for a review). Part of the variation in these prevalence estimates appears to be from substantial sample variation, discrepancies in the time frames referenced across studies (e.g., lifetime, past 12 months), references to different behaviors or categories of behaviors, and other methodological variation across studies (Peterson et al., 2011). Within this landscape, it can be difficult to select a primary estimate of the prevalence of male sexual assault. However, only a small number of survey-based sexual assault studies use nationally representative samples of civilians, and, of those, only one that included civilian men has been conducted in the past decade (see Farris et al., 2014, for a review). Fielded in 2011, the National Intimate Partner and Sexual Violence Survey used 21 behaviorally specific items to measure rape, attempted rape, and other sexual violence (Breiding et al., 2014). Based on this survey, the researchers estimated that 1.7 percent of men experienced an attempted or completed rape in their lifetime (compared with 19.3 percent of women). In addition, they estimated that 23.4 percent of men experienced other sexual violence (e.g., being made to penetrate someone else, sexual coercion, unwanted sexual contact) in their lifetime. Among women, 43.9 percent were estimated to have experienced other sexual violence in their lifetime.

As with civilian estimates, researchers studying military samples have reported a broad range of sexual assault rates for military men (from 0.02 percent to 12 percent) (Hoyt, Klosterman Rielage, and Williams, 2011). Again, respondent, definitional, and other methodological differences across studies likely explain much of the variation in prevalence estimates (Bachman, 2012; Farris et al., 2014; Fisher, 2004; Fisher and Cullen, 2000; Kilpatrick, 2004; National Research Council, 2014). For example, nonresponse rates across studies involving servicemen range from 3 percent to 92 percent, with particularly high nonresponse rates seen at the service academies; high nonresponse rates increase the possibility of inaccurate estimates. Further, some studies have used behaviorally specific items (e.g., touched, stroked, or fondled private areas[1]), and

---

[1]   *Private areas* typically include buttocks, inner thigh, breasts, groin, anus, vagina, penis, or testicles.

other studies have used legal terms (e.g., sexual assault) (Hoyt, Klosterman Rielage, and Williams, 2011). Overall, studies using data from anonymous surveys show a higher average rate of male sexual assault among U.S. military personnel (2.8 percent) than studies involving formal investigations of sexual assault (0.6 percent) (Hoyt, Klosterman Rielage, and Williams, 2011). And studies that use lifetime prevalence estimates, such as those that include childhood experiences of sexual assault, obtain higher estimates of male sexual assault among U.S. military personnel than studies that consider a more limited time frame (see, for example, Lapp et al., 2005).

One of the most recent assessments of sexual assault against military men was based on the 2014 RMWS (see Morral, Gore, and Schell, 2014), on which the 2016 WGRA methods are based. RAND designed the 2014 assessment to address criticisms in prior research on military sexual assault. For example, the study relied on a large representative sample, obtained an acceptable survey response rate, and used behaviorally specific survey items that aligned with the sexual assault criteria outlined in Article 120 of the UCMJ (see Morral, Gore, and Schell, 2014). The most recent fielding of the WGRA, in 2016, used these methods, and results showed that approximately 0.6 percent of active-duty men had experienced a sexual assault in the past year, with rates ranging from 0.3 percent in the Air Force to 0.9 percent in the Navy (Davis and Grifka, 2017a). For lifetime prevalence, 2.2 percent of active-duty men were estimated to have experienced a sexual assault in their lifetime, and 1.8 percent had experienced a sexual assault since joining the military (Davis and Grifka, 2017a).

Characteristics of Male Sexual Assault

Although less is known about the experiences of male victims of sexual assault than the experiences of female victims, an emerging literature has begun to coalesce around some basic facts and themes. As noted earlier, the WGRA now collects data from a large percentage of military servicemembers. It also uses state-of-the-art survey weights to correct for nonresponse bias (Davis, Falk, and Schneider, 2017; Ghosh-Dastidar et al., 2016). It is one of the first surveys to collect a large enough sample of male victims to allow analyses of the differences between men's and women's sexual assault experiences. Thus, even though research is limited, DoD has invested in the survey infrastructure necessary to provide needed data. The civilian literature is more often based on small and nonrepresentative samples of male victims (e.g., men who seek mental health services, men who report to law enforcement). In this section, we summarize the information from the DoD survey of servicemembers and contrast it with work on civilian victims to provide some context. This empirical information about the characteristics of male sexual assault provides background knowledge necessary to interpret relevant comments from our interviews with civilian experts specializing in male sexual assault and military providers who serve victims of sexual assault.

Perpetrator Characteristics

Some previous research on male sexual assault has considered perpetrator gender, number of offenders, relationship to victim, and other characteristics. In this section, we describe research on the characteristics of those who perpetrate male sexual assault.

Gender

Among male servicemembers who had been sexually assaulted in the past year, 69 percent indicated that their perpetrator was a man or that the group of people perpetrating the assault included both men and women (Severance, Debus, and Davis, 2017). This contrasts with female military victims, who were almost all (98 percent) assaulted by a man or by a group that included both men and women. The percentage of military male victims who reported being assaulted by male perpetrators (69 percent) appears to be lower than the percentage of civilian male victims who sought medical care: 93 percent of these civilians indicated that their perpetrator was a man (Stermac, del Bove, and Addison, 2004). Similarly, 86 percent of civilian male victims who reported an assault to civilian law enforcement indicated that the perpetrator was a man (Choudhary et al., 2012). This differentiation between civilian men and military men should be interpreted with caution. Civilian data are often drawn from help-seeking male victims, whereas the WGRA collects data from a representative sample of male servicemembers responding to a confidential survey that assesses all sexual assaults. Rather than reflecting a true distinction between civilian and military victims, the differences in these figures may reflect that sexual assaults requiring assistance from medical personnel or law enforcement are more often perpetrated by men.

Number of Offenders

A substantial proportion of sexual assaults against active-duty servicemen involve more than one perpetrator. Specifically, 33 percent of active-duty male sexual assault victims indicated that there were multiple offenders (Severance, Debus, and Davis, 2017). Among samples of civilian male sexual assault victims, the estimates vary greatly; 5 percent to 40 percent of male victims have indicated that there was more than one perpetrator (Bullock and Beckson, 2011; Isely and Gehrenbeck-Shim, 1997; McLean, 2013; Weiss, 2010). Furthermore, among civilian male victims, a larger proportion of male sexual assaults than female sexual assaults appear to involve more than one perpetrator, but this difference between military male and military female victims has varied over time and across studies (Bullock and Beckson, 2011; McLean, 2013; Morral, Gore, and Schell, 2014; Riggs et al., 2000; Severance, Debus, and Davis, 2017; Stermac, del Bove, and Addison, 2004; Weiss, 2010).

Relationship to the Victim

Among male servicemembers who were sexually assaulted in the past year, the largest proportion indicated that they were assaulted by a friend or acquaintance (43 percent), but many indicated that they were assaulted by a stranger (19 percent) or that they did not know who assaulted them (31 percent). Among male servicemembers who knew the military status of the offender(s), a large majority indicated that at least one offender was a member of the military (75 percent). Military male victims indicated that perpetrators who were military members were most often higher ranking than the victim (53 percent) or ranked similarly to the victim (40 percent). However, men (29 percent) were significantly more likely than women (19 percent) to have been assaulted by someone of lower rank (Severance, Debus, and Davis, 2017).

The military data are consistent with some research on civilian male victims of sexual assault. Using data from the National Incident-Based Reporting System (NIBRS), a multi-state criminological database of reported incidents in the United States, researchers found that most perpetrators of sexual assault against men were known to the victim (94 percent) (Choudhary et al., 2012). However, using data from the National Crime Victimization Survey (NCVS), Pino and Meier (1999) summarized data from 81 male sexual assault victims and found that the offender was most often a stranger (54 percent). The larger proportion of stranger assailants observed in the NCVS relative to the results seen among the military and NIBRS might be due to the NCVS's small sample size and its specific focus on rape (rather than all sexual assaults). Compared with female victims in the NCVS, male victims were more likely to be raped by a stranger (Pino and Meier, 1999).

Other Demographics

Beyond gender, military status, and relationship to the victim, the DoD WGRA does not assess other perpetrator characteristics (Davis et al., 2017). Among samples of civilian victims, most perpetrators of sexual assaults against men are white (69 percent to 80 percent) (Choudhary et al., 2012; Isely and Gehrenbeck-Shim, 1997; Pino and Meier, 1999), perceived to be heterosexual by their victims (90 percent) (Isely and Gehrenbeck-Shim, 1997), and under age 32 (Choudhary et al., 2012; Hodge and Canter, 1998; Pino and Meier, 1999).

Victim Characteristics

Research examining male sexual assault has also considered victim characteristics, including sexual orientation, gender identity, socioeconomic status, and prior victimization. In this section, we summarize findings from several previous studies on these topics.

Sexual Orientation and Gender Identity

In 2016, an assessment of sexual orientation and gender identity that had not been included in the RMWS was added to the WGRA, which allowed DoD to estimate relative risk for sexual assault for the first time among those of different sexual orientations (Davis et al., 2017). Based on this assessment, 3 percent of active-duty servicemen identified as gay, bisexual, or transgender (Davis, Vega, and McLeod, 2017).[2] These servicemen were substantially more likely to be sexually assaulted in the past year (3.5 percent) than were those who did not identify as gay, bisexual, or transgender (0.3 percent).

Among civilians, many, and likely most, victims of male sexual assault are heterosexual (Bullock and Beckson, 2011; Isely and Gehrenbeck-Shim, 1997; McLean, 2013). However, gay or bisexual men experience sexual assault at higher rates than heterosexual men (Bullock and Beckson, 2011; Langenderfer-Magruder et al., 2016), and a 2009 study found that approximately 50 percent of transgender persons had experienced unwanted sexual activity in their lifetime (Stotzer, 2009).

Socioeconomic Status

Pay grade is a marker of income in the military, but it is also associated with organizational power and, usually, with age. Thus, the comparison between household income among civilians and pay grades among servicemembers is not exactly parallel. Nonetheless, data show that enlisted servicemen in lower pay grades are more likely than those in higher pay grades to be sexually assaulted (Severance, Debus, and Davis, 2017). Among civilians, research suggests that most male victims in the United States are from a household with an income of either $25,000–$74,999 (50 percent) or less than $25,000 (46.4 percent) (Isely and Gehrenbeck-Shim, 1997; Weiss, 2010).

Other Demographics

Among active-duty servicemen who experienced a sexual assault in the past year, most were under age 30 (71 percent), white (56 percent), and in junior enlisted pay grades (67 percent). Relative to servicemen who were not sexually assaulted in the past year, those who were assaulted were significantly younger, were less likely to be African-American, were in lower pay grades, and had higher Armed Forces Qualifying Test scores (Severance, Debus, and Davis, 2017).

Notably, much of the research addressing military sexual assault among U.S. military veterans assesses a broad category of experiences labeled *military sexual trauma* (MST). MST, as defined by U.S. Department of Veterans Affairs (VA) screening questions, includes experiencing sexual contact via threat or force or experiencing unwanted sexual attention (e.g., touching, pressuring for sexual favors) while in the military (Maguen et al., 2012). Among veterans who deployed in Operation Enduring Freedom or Operation Iraqi Freedom and sought care at a VA facility, most men who screened positive for MST were aged 18 to 34 (61 percent) and were non-Hispanic white (64 percent) (Kimerling et al., 2010). Almost half of these men were married (49 percent). In terms of military service characteristics, 72 percent of the men who screened positive for MST served in the Army. Furthermore, 53 percent of the men who screened positive were on active duty, and 95 percent served in the enlisted grades.

---

[2]   Categorization as "servicemen" was based on self-report in the survey.

When considering male civilians, research indicates that most victims are non-Hispanic white (Isely and Gehrenbeck-Shim, 1997; Weiss, 2010). However, risk appears to be higher among African-American men relative to white men (Choudhary et al., 2012). In addition, the average age of adult male sexual assault victims who are civilians is between 20 and 30 years (Bullock and Beckson, 2011; Isely and Gehrenbeck-Shim, 1997; McLean, 2013; Stermac, del Bove, and Addison, 2004; Weiss, 2010).

Prior Sexual Victimization

Overall, both men and women with a history of childhood sexual abuse are at higher risk for experiencing sexual assault as an adult (Hines, 2007). One study found that men who experienced sexual assault in adulthood were five times more likely to have a history of childhood sexual assault than men who had not experienced sexual assault in adulthood, and these childhood experiences appeared to amplify trauma-related symptoms following an adult sexual assault (e.g., anxiety, depression, irritability) (Elliott, Mok, and Briere, 2004; see also Stermac, del Bove, and Addison, 2004). The reasons why those who experience sexual assault in adulthood are more likely to have a history of childhood sexual assault are not yet clear.

Researchers have noted that many individuals, particularly men, may enlist in the military in an effort to escape adversity (Blosnich et al., 2014). Research involving active-component U.S. personnel, members of the National Guard and Reserves, and U.S. military veterans has shown that men who experienced sexual assault during military service had a greater number of instances of childhood sexual abuse, childhood physical abuse, and traumatic life events (Martin, Rosen, and Durand, 1998; Murdoch, Polusny, Street, et al., 2014; Schry et al., 2015). This corresponds with research involving community samples (Hines, 2007). According to the 2016 WGRA, 0.9 percent of active-component men and 6.8 percent of active-component women experienced at least one sexual assault before joining the military (Davis and Grifka, 2017a).

Assault Characteristics

In addition to examining the characteristics of the perpetrators and victims of male sexual assault, studies have examined the characteristics of the assaults themselves. In this section, we review some of the findings from these studies.

Type

Several studies have considered the types of sexual assaults against men. Using DoD definitions, *penetrative* sexual assaults include penetration of the mouth or anus by an object, penis, or body part. *Nonpenetrative* assaults include sexual contact with private areas of the servicemember's body or incidents in which the servicemember is forced to touch the private areas of someone else's body. *Attempted penetrative* assaults are those in which someone attempted to sexually assault the servicemember, but there was no contact with a private area (such contact would have allowed classification as a nonpenetrative sexual assault).

Among servicemen who had been sexually assaulted in the past year, approximately one-third experienced a penetrative sexual assault (35 percent), and two-thirds experienced a nonpenetrative or attempted penetrative assault (65 percent) (Davis and Grifka, 2017a).

The majority of sexual assaults perpetrated against civilian men involve penetrative anal assault (Bullock and Beckson, 2011; Hillman et al., 1991; Isely and Gehrenbeck-Shim, 1997; McLean, 2013; Stermac, del Bove, and Addison, 2004). Across civilian studies, forced fellatio was involved in approximately 20 percent to 60 percent of male sexual assaults (Isely and Gehrenbeck-Shim, 1997; Stermac, del Bove, and Addison, 2004). Fondling, either performed on the victim or that the victim was forced to perform on the perpetrator, was reported in 20 percent to 55 percent of civilian male sexual assaults (Choudhary et al., 2012; Isely and Gehrenbeck-Shim, 1997; Stermac, del Bove, and Addison, 2004). Although it appears that civilian male victims are more likely than military victims to experience a penetrative assault, note that the military sample is a representative sample of male victims, while the civilian studies typically describe male victims who seek help or report the assault. Because help-seeking is associated with severity, we would expect that samples of help-seeking men would be characterized by more-severe assaults.

Prior to being categorized as having experienced a sexual assault, servicemembers who participated in the 2014 RMWS responded to screening items about the type of unwanted sexual contact they had experienced.[3] Among servicemen who responded that they had experienced at least one of the items, the most common experiences were being touched on their private areas or forced to touch someone else's private areas; penetration by an object, penis, or other body part was less common, and being forced to penetrate someone else was least common (Jaycox, Schell, Morral, et al., 2015).

Tactics

For military victims, the 2014 RMWS included a series of questions assessing the offender's tactics (e.g., use of physical force, threats) (Jaycox, Schell, Farris, et al., 2014), and the results from this question were not provided in the overview report for the 2016 WGRA. The sample of male victims who responded to these questions in the 2014 RMWS was too small to accurately estimate the percentage of offenders who employed each type of assault tactic in penetrative assaults (Jaycox, Schell, Morral, et al., 2015). However, for nonpenetrative assaults, the most common offender tactic was continuing even after the male victim told or showed the offender that he was unwilling (61 percent). Threating the victim (16 percent) and use of physical force (14 percent) were the next most common tactics but occurred during substantially fewer nonpenetrative assaults (Jaycox, Schell, Morral, et al., 2015).

---

[3] The results from this question were not provided in the most recent overview report on the 2016 WGRA (Davis et al., 2017).

For civilians, perpetrator use of physical violence, physical restraint, or physical threats appears to be involved in approximately 40 percent or more of male sexual assaults (Choudhary et al., 2012; McLean, 2013; Stermac, del Bove, and Addison, 2004). Offender physical violence appears to be more common and more severe during sexual assaults against civilian men relative to women (Pino and Meier, 1999; Tewksbury, 2007). Weapons are involved in 10 percent or fewer of male sexual assaults (Choudhary et al., 2012; McLean, 2013; Weiss, 2010).

The majority of sexual assaults against civilian and military men do not involve alcohol or drug consumption by the victim or assailant (Choudhary et al., 2012; Weiss, 2010; Severance, Debus, and Davis, 2017). Such use, when it is involved, appears to be even less common when the perpetrator is a stranger than when the perpetrator is known (Stermac, del Bove, and Addison, 2004). Some researchers have speculated that male sexual assault victims may underreport use of substances but do not suggest why these victims may underreport (Choudhary et al., 2012).

Location

More than 40 percent of civilian male victims are assaulted in a residence (Choudhary et al., 2012; Isely and Gehrenbeck-Shim, 1997; Weiss, 2010). By contrast, a smaller proportion of military male victims report being assaulted in a residence (25 percent) (Severance, Debus, and Davis, 2017). In addition, most active-duty male victims reported being sexually assaulted at a military installation or aboard a military ship (64 percent). About half were assaulted at their workplace during duty hours (45 percent), and 31 percent were assaulted while out with friends or at a party. Compared with female victims, male victims were significantly less likely to have been assaulted while off base, out with friends, or in someone else's home. Male victims were significantly more likely than female victims to be assaulted while on temporary duty, on temporary additional duty, at sea, at a military function, or at work during duty hours, as well as during field exercise alerts or an overseas port visit (Severance, Debus, and Davis, 2017).

Injuries

During sexual assaults, approximately 30 percent to 40 percent of civilian male victims are physically injured, typically in the perineal or anal area (McLean, 2013; Stermac, del Bove, and Addison, 2004), and 6 percent to 9 percent require medical attention (Stermac, del Bove, and Addison, 2004; Weiss, 2010). Among civilian victims who reported the assault to law enforcement, younger male victims appeared to have higher injury rates than male victims aged 30 or older (Choudhary et al., 2012). For military victims of male sexual assault, about one-half indicated that they were injured during the assault, but the type of injury was not assessed (Morral, Gore, and Schell, 2014). Assault-related injuries were more common among servicemen relative to women (Morral, Gore, and Schell, 2014).

Erection or Ejaculation During the Assault

An involuntary erection and ejaculation during sexual assault can occur for some male victims (Bullock and Beckson, 2011). For example, some men may experience an erection during times of intense fear or pain (Tewksbury, 2007). In addition, victims may intentionally ejaculate to minimize the assault duration, or offenders may make the victim ejaculate as a strategy to confuse the victim and discourage reporting (Fuchs, 2004). Research on arousal and ejaculation during a male sexual assault is limited, and no data are available on prevalence in a military sample. Among civilian victims, one study found that 18 percent of male victims who accessed sexual assault counseling services were stimulated to ejaculation (King and Woollett, 1997). Research reinforces that victim arousal or ejaculation is not indicative of victim consent (e.g., Bullock and Beckson, 2011; Fuchs, 2004).

Hazing

The RMWS assessment of sexual assault was specifically designed to ensure that men who were assaulted as part of a hazing incident would be included in the assessment (Jaycox, Schell, Farris, et al., 2014). Because neither the assailant nor victim in hazing sexual assaults may perceive the event to be sexual in nature, the screening items were designed to avoid using the words *sex* or *sexual*. For respondents who experienced an unwanted penetrative or nonpenetrative contact event, follow-up questions categorized the event as a sexual assault if the respondent indicated that the intent was to abuse or humiliate them or was for a sexual purpose. Drawing from the most recent reported estimates, military male victims (70 percent) were far more likely than military female victims (42 percent) to indicate that the assault was intended to abuse or humiliate them (Jaycox, Schell, Morral, et al., 2015). Other suggestions that male military sexual assault victims are more likely than female victims to be assaulted as part of hazing events include the fact that a greater proportion of male victims (45 percent) are more likely than female victims (27 percent) to indicate that the assault took place at work during duty hours (Davis and Grifka, 2017b). Finally, military male victims (26 percent) are more than twice as likely as female victims (10 percent) to label their worst sexual assault in the past year as a hazing incident (Severance, Debus, and Davis, 2017). Researchers note that "together, these differences suggest a pattern in which sexual assaults against men often involve repeated, physically violent assaults that occur in a context of bullying, abuse, or hazing, often perpetrated by multiple coworkers in their workplace" (Jaycox, Schell, Morral, et al., 2015, p. 90).

For civilians, preliminary qualitative studies suggest that some sexual assaults against adult, civilian men are hazing-related. For example, more-senior members of groups or sports teams may sexually assault junior members as part of hazing rituals in order to assert the position of the junior members at the bottom of the hierarchy (Anderson, McCormack, and Lee, 2012; Kirby and Wintrup, 2002). However, we are not aware of any studies that estimate the proportion of male sexual assaults among civilians that are hazing-related.

Summary

In this chapter, we summarized what is known about victim, perpetrator, and assault characteristics of sexual assaults against men. The best-available research suggests that 1.7 percent of civilian men have experienced a completed or attempted rape in their lifetime, and 2.6 percent of military men have experienced a sexual assault in their lifetime.[4] Based on the estimates of annual prevalence, in a room of 100 servicemen, the odds suggest that one will be sexually assaulted in the coming year. Although continuing to improve measurement precision may provide the data necessary to better target response resources to those in need, there is no longer a question that a large number of military servicemen have been victims of sexual assault. In the next chapter, we discuss needs that these men might have.

---

[4] The civilian estimate excludes nonpenetrative sexual assaults, while the military estimate includes them.

CHAPTER THREE

Identifying and Addressing the Needs of Male Sexual Assault Victims

To better address the needs of servicemen who have been sexually assaulted, it is necessary to first understand what those needs are and then ensure that service providers are appropriately trained to address the identified needs. In this chapter, we describe insights regarding victim needs that we learned from our interviews with civilian experts and military service providers and draw from related literature on the short- and long-term needs that male victims may have after a sexual assault.

Perceived Needs of Victims

We interviewed a variety of civilian experts and military service providers to uncover the range of services and support that male victims may need. Notably, sexual assault victims may seek different support services from different professionals. For example, they may choose to discuss their legal needs, but not mental health symptoms, with their legal counsel. The results of our analyses showed some variation by interviewee profession in terms of needs discussed. However, across interviewees of different professions, the following were discussed as needs of all sexual assault victims and of male victims specifically: mental health care, advocacy, chain-of-command support, social support, information, legal support, and medical care (Appendix B, Tables B.1 and B.2). More interviewees discussed mental health care needs than any other need, and medical care needs were raised least often. The limited discussion of medical care needs among interviewees could be attributed to multiple factors, including delays in help-seeking until after physical symptoms have resolved and the limited number of physical health (e.g., medical) service providers in our sample.

When we asked military service providers to compare the needs of male and female sexual assault victims in the military, they perceived that there were some differences in needs between men and women (see Table B.3). When discussing these differences, service providers tended to discuss gender differences in the barriers to accessing needed services rather than differences in the types of services needed. These barriers for men included greater concerns over stigma and reluctance to report.

We heard similar descriptions from the civilian experts we interviewed. For example, three of the five experts who commented on this topic observed that the resources for male and female victims may not need to be different, but they may need to be provided in ways that are accepting of and accessible to male victims. One civilian expert commented, "what needs to be different is that there's an awareness that men are safe [accessing services] too." Another echoed this sentiment, stating, "I don't actually know if there's different resources needed other than . . . [providers] need to be very well trained in understanding men's perspectives as victims."

Several civilian interviewees also highlighted that victims' needs are highly variable, depending on their personal situation and their reasons for coming forward. One expert noted, for example, that it is more important to understand the individual needs of each victim who is seeking help than to focus on average gender differences.

In the next sections, we provide more information on several of the categories of needs that our interviewees discussed, including previous research relevant to these categories, as well as observations and quotations from the interviewees.

Advocacy, Social Support, and Information

According to research with civilians, male sexual assault victims may isolate themselves from others, including emotionally distancing themselves and withdrawing from their social network (Walker, Archer, and Davies, 2005). Previous research showed that, among veterans who had been referred to a mental health clinic for anxiety, those who had experienced MST (1) perceived less support from those in their social network than those who had not experienced MST and (2) were more likely to indicate that they have been "shamed, embarrassed, or repeatedly told [they were] no good" (Mondragon et al., 2015).

Although support persons can come from a victim's informal network (e.g., a friend or parent), some victims do not have a sympathetic and knowledgeable support person in their social network. To ensure that all military sexual assault victims have immediate access to advocacy, social support, and information, each service branch's Sexual Assault Prevention and Response (SAPR) or Sexual Harassment/Assault Response and Prevention program includes victim advocates who are available to guide victims through reporting decisions, provide information about available services, accompany the victim to post-assault medical or legal appointments, address immediate safety needs, and offer support (DoD, 2013). DoD also offers Safe Helpline, which provides confidential crisis counseling, information about services and reporting choices, and support (Safe Helpline, undated-a).

Support services may be particularly important to male victims. Four of the military service providers we interviewed believed that male sexual assault victims have less social support and experience more shame than female victims (Table B.3). One military service provider for the Army commented,

> I think males may be more concerned about loss of masculinity, and therefore they need somebody to listen to them that's not going to make them feel like they're somehow less of a man because they allowed this to happen to them. Whereas, for females, there's a different kind of loss that they experience—safety, security—and they tend to feel like it's their fault. And so they need to know, "Hey, it's not your fault. No matter what you did, you didn't ask for this," and so on and so forth, that narrative. A male may very well need to hear, "Look, you're not any less of a man. You're not any less of a person because a woman did this to you or another man did this to you. Nothing's been taken from you except your right to be safe, your right to not be violated." Stuff like that.[1]

Support Related to Sexual Identity Concerns

Both previous research and comments from our interviewees suggest that male victims may need support to process concerns about sexual identity and loss of masculinity that can arise following a sexual assault. Research with civilian men reveals that some heterosexual victims are concerned or even fearful that they will be perceived as gay because of the sexual assault, and some gay victims can feel as though the assault was punishment for their sexual orientation (Davies, 2002; Gold, Marx, and Lexington, 2007; Isely and Gehrenbeck-Shim, 1997; Peterson et al., 2011; Tewksbury, 2007). For both heterosexual and gay men, sexual assault can lead to long-term confusion or concerns about their sexual identity (Isely, 1998; Tewksbury, 2007; Walker, Archer, and Davies, 2005). One civilian mental health care provider commented,

> Men struggle much more with their sense of their own masculinity after an assault, because we really don't ever talk about or hear about male survivors. So that, for them, it's a real threat to their masculinity, and they may not even feel like men anymore. . . . That also gets in the way of their ability to seek help because they feel weak and less manly if they . . . get help for their struggles.
>
> . . . Another core struggle is with sexual orientation. . . . [The assault] may cause them to question their sexual orientation or feel like they're to blame somehow for the assault.

The desire for additional research on the specific needs of transgender victims was also highlighted by a mental health care provider for the Navy, who told us, "Addressing the needs of transgender individuals . . . may be something to focus on. . . . Certainly, one of my fears is that these individuals will be a target by predators."

---

[1] Per this interviewee's request, we do not state the interviewee's occupation.

Comments that emphasized male-specific concerns regarding sexuality and identity suggest that these might be areas where DoD should provide additional support. These concerns include confusion among heterosexual victims about whether an involuntary erection means that they are gay and confusion among all male victims about whether an involuntary erection could mean that they had consented. Service providers also addressed the self-blame that male victims may experience. One provider of physical health care services for the Marine Corps commented,

> There's so many of them, regardless of the way they identify themselves with their sexual orientation, regardless of which way that they lean, they tend to really, really blame themselves. Because guys just, for whatever reason, they just seem to think they should've been able to stop it. And so, because of that, they really doubt themselves.

Mental Health Care

In this section, we review the literature on mental and behavioral health care needs of male sexual assault victims and then describe insights from our interviewees. According to the published literature on civilian sexual assaults, a large proportion of male sexual assault victims experience symptoms of depression, anxiety, nightmares, flashbacks, self-blame, low self-esteem, or problems with anger control following the assault (Isely and Gehrenbeck-Shim, 1997; Walker, Archer, and Davies, 2005). Among military veterans who sought care at a VA facility, men and women who had experienced MST had higher odds of posttraumatic stress disorder (PTSD), other anxiety disorders, and depression than veterans who were not victims of MST during their military career (Kimerling et al., 2010; Maguen et al., 2012). Research focusing specifically on male veterans has shown that men who experienced MST, or sexual assault specifically, self-reported a greater number of depression symptoms and were more likely to be diagnosed with a mood disorder than were men who had not had these experiences (Chang et al., 2003; Mondragon et al., 2015). Male victims, whether civilian or military, may experience suicidal ideation, and some may make a suicide attempt (Schry et al., 2015; Tiet, Finney, and Moos, 2006; Walker, Archer, and Davies, 2005). Male veterans with a history of sexual assault report more difficulty controlling their anger and more nightmares and flashbacks than male veterans without this history (Cucciare et al., 2011).

In addition, alcohol abuse, drug abuse, and increased use of tobacco are commonly reported among male sexual assault victims (Cook et al., 2016; Guina et al., 2016; Isely and Gehrenbeck-Shim, 1997; Peterson et al., 2011; Walker, Archer, and Davies, 2005). Among military veterans who sought care at a VA facility, men and women who had experienced MST had higher odds of substance use disorders than veterans who had not experienced MST (Kimerling et al., 2010; Maguen et al., 2012). In addition, male veterans with a history of sexual assault reported higher levels of consumption of alcohol and multiple drugs—including heroin, sedatives, cocaine, meth-amphetamines, hallucinogens, and inhalants—than male veterans without this history (Cucciare et al., 2011).

Some men may be at higher risk for mental health problems following a sexual assault than others. Men who believe or endorse male sexual assault myths (see Chapter Five) may have particular difficulty coping. In examining risk for mental health symptoms, Voller and colleagues (2015) found that higher rape myth acceptance and sexual victimization in the past were associated with decreased self-efficacy among male sexual assault victims. Self-efficacy, in turn, was negatively associated with psychiatric symptoms.

One commonly held misunderstanding about male sexual assault victims has been that men are not as negatively affected by sexual assault as women are (Peterson et al., 2011). However, the mental health symptoms for which male victims are at increased risk correspond with the same symptoms often experienced by female victims (Ullman and Filipas, 2001). In fact, most research suggests that male sexual assault victims react at least as negatively as female victims do. A study that relied on a stratified random sample of the U.S. population found that men with a history of adult sexual assault demonstrated more trauma-related symptoms than women with a history of adult sexual assault did in the following domains: anxious arousal, depression, intrusive experiences, defensive avoidance, dissociation, sexual concerns, dysfunctional sexual behavior, impaired self-reference, and tension reduction behaviors (Elliott, Mok, and Briere, 2004). Research also suggests that male victims of sexual assault react with more hostility and anger than female victims do (Frazier, 1993; Walker, Archer, and Davies, 2005).

For male sexual assault victims who develop psychiatric conditions, such as major depressive disorder or PTSD, evidence-based treatments for these conditions are available. VA/DoD Clinical Practice Guidelines for posttraumatic stress, major depressive disorder, and other conditions provide strong recommendations for effective psycho-pharmacological or behavioral therapies that can help servicemen recover from these conditions (Management of Major Depressive Disorder Working Group, 2016; Management of Post-Traumatic Stress Working Group, 2010). Although experimental, non-validated treatments that are specific to male sexual assault victims should continue to be tested, victims should be informed that the treatments are experimental and should be offered access to validated treatments for any behavioral health conditions that they are experiencing.

Limited research has assessed the efficacy of mental health treatment specifically designed to assist male sexual assault victims. Hoyt, Klosterman Rielage, and Williams (2012) evaluated a group-based treatment protocol for addressing interpersonal and psychological issues among male veterans who have experienced MST. The three-phase group therapy addressed interpersonal effectiveness, self-esteem and forgiveness, and the integration of new skills and beliefs into participants' lives. Only two of 11 participants completed treatment, and PTSD symptoms declined for both of them.

Although this group-based treatment for sexual assault–related conditions might assist with addressing mental health symptoms among male sexual assault victims in the U.S. military, the small sample prevents strong conclusions regarding the utility of this treatment for this population.

Cognitive processing therapy, an evidence-based treatment for PTSD (Management of Post-Traumatic Stress Working Group, 2010), has also been evaluated among male veterans who experienced MST. Using archival data to assess the effect of a residential treatment program using cognitive processing therapy, researchers found significant decreases in PTSD and depression symptoms among male veterans who had experienced MST (Voelkel et al., 2015). In a separate study of cognitive processing therapy delivered in an outpatient setting, 11 male veterans with a history of MST showed significant declines in PTSD and depressive symptoms following therapy (Mullen et al., 2014). Improvements were maintained for at least 6 months after treatment completion.

Most sexual assault victims will not develop a psychiatric condition that requires specialized treatment, but some may desire mental health care for subclinical trauma-related symptoms. In this case, researchers and clinicians have proposed that different issues may need to be addressed depending on whether the victim is seeking treatment soon after the assault or long after the assault, such as years later (Vearnals and Campbell, 2001). Early psychological treatment for sexual assault–related conditions may include providing a supportive context for male victims to talk about the assault and address concerns regarding their masculinity and feelings of anger and shame, along with trauma-related symptoms. Later treatment may involve cognitive-behavioral therapy or similar approaches to address sexual identity concerns, intrusive thoughts, and symptoms of PTSD or depression (Vearnals and Campbell, 2001).

Perceptions of Male Victim Mental Health Care Needs

Those we interviewed distinguished the immediate crisis intervention needs that male victims may have immediately following an assault from longer-term follow-up needs, and many interviewees had suggestions for how care can be tailored to the needs of male sexual assault survivors.

The most frequently mentioned comment made by military service providers regarding resources needed for male sexual assault victims was that the military system needs additional male-specific mental health services, such as men's support groups and counselors with greater knowledge of the needs of male sexual assault victims (see Table B.18 for more detail). A provider of physical health services to Navy personnel commented,

> I'd like to see more support groups for the men, . . . groups of four and five so that they can realize they're not alone, basically. You know, the male attacks tend to be more violent, tend to be more aggressive, and I just think that it would be nice to see support groups for them that are not a group of 20 but maybe a group of four

or five connected. I think they would respond better to that . . . . Even [video tele-conference] support groups for guys, where they're not sitting next to each other but [it is] connecting them through a phone conference where they can talk and no one knows who they are. I think that might be very helpful.

Among the civilian experts we talked with, opinion was divided about the value of group-based therapy relative to individual therapy for male victims of sexual assault. Some believed that it was critical for male victims to be exposed to other men who had a similar experience. For example, one civilian mental health care provider noted,

> Individual therapy is fine, but men especially need to talk to other men. . . . Then they no longer feel like a freak, and they no longer feel like they were weak and sick. And they actually start to feel like, "Wow, I can have self-esteem again. I can thrive." . . . A therapist can help with that to a large degree, but I think having a group experience and being able to talk to other men is really critical.

Another civilian mental health care provider commented that the value of group-based therapy is also possible via cyber interventions. Discussing an online support group for victims, the interviewee noted,

> They get first-stage psychoeducation. They get . . . [to] know each other by their nicknames. They say stuff like, "Hey, I've been there" or "I got your back, bro." It's really lovely stuff that you hear in brick and mortar work. . . . It's not the full monte of service provisions to survivors, but wow, what a useful first step.

A third such provider, however, expressed reservations about male treatment groups, commenting,

> I want to say that group therapy for male survivors is important and probably a resource that's less available than it should be. The thing that's hanging me up is that many men don't want to do that, so part of the reason why there aren't as many groups for men is probably because it's hard to recruit enough men to run a group. . . . For some men, it's the shame and embarrassment. Just the idea of having a group of people know that about them is too aversive.

And finally, another civilian mental health care provider succinctly summarized the two perspectives by pointing to the need for individualized care:

> I think some research is needed on men's treatment preferences. People tend to assume that men want certain kinds of mental health treatment. For example, they only want individual treatment, or they never want to do a group, or they must have a long-term support group, or they can only work with female clinicians not male clinicians. And the truth is their preferences really are actually diverse, and there's no one-size-fits-all.

Career Support

The experience of MST among men serving in the military is strongly associated with military separation or retirement (Millegan et al., 2016). The military service providers we interviewed brought up the career support that victims may need, particularly support from their chain of command. As one Navy mental health care provider described it,

> [It's] a lot of anxiety, a lot of depression, also dealing with the anger and the self-blaming that can come along with that, and other mental health issues that can be exaggerated because of the environment. Often, [it's] not having the opportunity to address those mental health issues because of the [operations] tempo. If things are at a fast pace, you may not allow yourself to get the treatment that you need because you want to be really gung ho and help the team. And you want to be mission first and not allow yourself to sit still and feel what you're feeling, so you try to bottle up whatever feelings you have.

A victim's chain of command can support the victim's needs in a variety of ways, including supporting access to services, which may require appointments during work hours. As one mental health care provider for the Air Force described,

> Primarily what [victims] are looking for from command is just support. So, allowing them to attend medical and mental health appointments as needed; reassignment if that's something that they desire or something that everyone agrees would be in the victim's best interest. And so, primarily [they need] support.

Medical Care

Research with civilians (Tewksbury, 2007) and servicemembers (Jaycox, Schell, Morral, et al., 2015) suggests that, when compared with sexual assaults against women, sexual assaults against men are more likely to be violent, are more likely to involve a weapon, and are associated with more corollary injuries. However, as discussed in more detail in Chapter Four, male victims appear to be reluctant to seek help (Masho and Alvanzo, 2009; Monk-Turner and Light, 2010; Severance, Debus, and Davis, 2017). Therefore, it is likely that only the victims with the most-pressing injuries receive immediate medical care. Among civilian male victims who did seek emergency department care, 25 percent to 64 percent had experienced a traumatic injury during the assault (Pesola, Westfal, and Kuffner, 1999; Riggs et al., 2000; Stermac, del Bove, and Addison, 2004). Common injuries include soft-tissue injuries; genital or anal abrasions and tears; and bruising on the head, neck, or face (Ernst et al., 2000; Riggs et al., 2000; Stermac, del Bove, and Addison, 2004). Long-term physical health consequences can include sexually transmitted infections (Hillman et al., 1991), sexual dysfunction (Peterson et al., 2011; Tewksbury, 2007), tension headaches, ulcers, and colitis (Tewksbury, 2007).

Similar to civilian men, male veterans with a history of MST have significantly higher odds of having a diagnosis of a sexually transmitted infection, sexual desire disorder, or sexual arousal disorder than military men without this MST history (Turchik, Pavao, Nazarian, et al., 2012).

Our interviews with civilian and military experts did not touch often on medical care needs among victims. One civilian interviewee noted the research showing that male victims experience more-violent assaults with greater risk of injury and added that this will affect "what sort of injuries and what sort of mental and physical trauma need to be attended to." A civilian mental health care provider added, "There might be some unique things, like the physical damage after an assault, that could lead to long-term problems with rectal pain if they were anally sexually assaulted, erectile dysfunction, or difficulties with sexual functioning."

Other Needs

Interviewees noted that male victims may also have legal, spiritual, or financial needs following an assault, but these needs were not discussed in as much detail as those previously described. In addition, military service providers discussed victims' concerns about, and need for, privacy. Commenting on this, a Navy mental health care provider stated,

> The privacy is a big piece because a lot of the reason that people don't report in the military is because they worry about their privacy, and they expect things to be spoken about amongst the command. So, helping them understand that you're not here to talk about their information with others, that you're able to protect their rights and support them through the process and not just go talk about it with anyone who does not have a need to know—those are some important things, I think.

We discuss privacy concerns in greater detail in the next chapter.

Meeting Male Victim Needs Through Provider Preparation

Male victims often seek help for a variety of individualized needs, ranging from short-term advocacy and medical health care to longer-term mental health support. Military service providers working in the sexual assault, medical, mental health, chaplaincy, and legal fields may already have training to support female victims that can be readily translated to care for male victims. In other cases, additional training in addressing the unique needs of male victims or in ensuring a sensitive, gender-specific approach toward men may be necessary. To summarize providers' preparation to meet the needs of male sexual assault victims in the military, we reviewed the published literature on provider recommendations and asked our interviewees about their perceptions of provider preparation and training needs.

Researchers recommend that the curriculum used to train military service providers include factual information about male sexual assault and address common myths about sexual assault against men and women (Anderson and Quinn, 2009; Kassing and Prieto, 2003). If service providers build a factual foundation of information about male sexual assault and understand the potential impact of false beliefs on male victims, they will be in a better position to counter the harmful rape myths that victims may believe about themselves (e.g., "I should have been able to stop it") and that others might believe about them (Davies, 2002). Research examining the attitudes and perceptions of counselors in training found that, overall, these individuals did not clearly reject myths regarding sexual assault, but, notably, those who had completed a larger number of training sessions were less likely to blame a male sexual victim for being assaulted (Kassing and Prieto, 2003).

In addition to recommending training that reduces endorsement of male sexual assault myths, researchers recommend several ways that service providers should interact with male sexual assault victims. For example, researchers advise providers to establish a good rapport when a victim initially comes forward and suggest using normalizing statements, such as "Everyone takes time to deal with an assault" (Tomlinson and Harrison, 1998, p. 721). Researchers also recommend assessing the victim's potential coping ability—for example, by asking about available support networks and victim perceptions of himself and others (Tomlinson and Harrison, 1998). Service providers should also be aware that even clients with strong social networks may encounter negative reactions and a lack of support after an assault (Davies, 2002).

Furthermore, medical professionals may need specialized training in forensic examination of men's bodies (Scarce, 1997), and advocates and mental health care providers should be aware of and sensitive to some male victims' confusion regarding sexual identity (Turchik, Pavao, Hyun, et al., 2012). Availability and understanding of legal recourse for male sexual assault victims might assist with increasing victim reporting. Therefore, service providers might work to ensure or increase provision of straightforward information on the legal system, legal timelines and processes, and victim's rights. However, systematic research considering public awareness and attitudes toward the legal system and how those affect reporting and case attrition has focused on female sexual assault victims (e.g., Campbell, 2005; Frazier and Haney, 1996). There is no available information regarding the extent to which perceptions of the legal system affect male victim reporting or the long-term psychological consequences of case attrition among male victims who do report.

Perceptions of Service Provider Preparation

We asked the civilian experts we interviewed which groups would benefit from additional training on male victims of sexual assault. Some interviewees commented on the range of providers who interact with victims and who thus could benefit in some way from additional training; those providers included, for example, therapists, health care providers, spiritual support personnel, physicians and nurses, substance abuse treatment providers, and the staff of rape crisis organizations. Suggestions for training topics included information about why men have trouble seeking help, information about the scope of the problem (i.e., the number of male victims), and strategies to avoid making assumptions when working with sexual assault victims (e.g., about the gender of a victim or perpetrator, about mental health consequences for a given victim). When describing how training service providers can affect barriers to male victims coming forward, one civilian mental health care provider stated,

> I think the biggest difference . . . is talking about socialization issues and the impact of those messages. Helping people understand why men are so blocked from being able to come forward. Once you do actual treatment, there's not too much difference. I think . . . one thing that's important in treatment is really helping shore up a man's masculinity and helping them understand that they do have strength and they do have courage, because they believe the contrary—that being a victim means that they're powerless and helpless and no longer a man. So helping them affirm their masculinity, to me, is a really important difference in doing the work.

Among the military service providers we spoke to about this topic, most believed that individuals in their profession were either somewhat informed or well informed about sexual assault against men in the military.[2] However, this was not consistent across all professions. Specifically, only two chaplains believed that those in the chaplaincy were somewhat informed or well informed about assisting male victims (Table B.25). In response to being asked how well prepared military chaplains were to serve male victims, an Army chaplain stated, "I think I could sell it very short and say not very. And I think that's true from a models standpoint. We're not taught any models anywhere in the Army for modalities for treating survivors of sexual assault."

Among military service providers who discussed the extent to which their training addressed male sexual assault, interviewees provided mixed responses. Almost half of those who responded recalled that their training provided either some information or a good deal of information on male sexual assault (Table B.26). They mentioned videos that addressed male victims, vignettes that included male victims, talks from male sexual assault survivors or organizations that advocate for male victims (e.g., MaleSurvivor.org), and materials that included descriptive statistics on male victims in the military. However, slightly more than half of those who responded recalled

---

[2] When we summarize interviewee comments, the terms *most* and *majority* indicate that more than half of those who commented on a specific topic or responded to a particular question provided comments that were coded as the referenced theme. For more information, see Appendixes B and C.

that their training provided little or no information on male sexual assault. All of the chaplains who responded described their training as either minimally addressing male sexual assault or not addressing it at all.

Most service providers who addressed training needs believed that more training on male sexual assault would be helpful (Table B.27). The most frequently discussed desire was for more information on how to counsel and appropriately interact with male sexual assault victims (Table B.28). An Army legal counselor explained,

> We all know how to be lawyers; we know how to do the legal piece of this job. And this job in particular requires you to do a lot that's extra-legal. . . . We take great pains not to try to be therapists; we absolutely don't try to get in that lane. But let's be honest: These people have very unique traumatic issues. They're survivors of horrible things. And so, you've got to be sensitive, and you have to know how to talk to people, and you have to ideally have some kind of framework to draw from when you're advising them.

Relatedly, eight service providers expressed a desire to learn more about the psychological effects of sexual assault on male victims and to hear from male sexual assault victims during training. Addressing the need for more information on psychological effects, one Army chaplain said,

> I would say probably [training] would help us, even if the majority of it is more understanding about what is happening in the mind of somebody who's been assaulted in that way. What are their needs? . . . It could be that some [men] have a stronger . . . need for security than identity. The bottom line is I think that we would certainly benefit from some additional training.

However, 15 of the service providers who commented on this topic believed that additional training was not needed. They pointed to the low base rates of male sexual assault and noted that they would likely provide services to only a small number of male victims during their careers. Explaining this viewpoint, one mental health care provider for the Air Force stated,

> I'm not sure what the incremental validity would be of having specific training for mental health providers. We train on an awful lot of things. We have trainings on top of trainings. That's not to say that this is not important. It certainly is. It's just I would wonder about the return on investment. Because every time something comes up, some sort of low base rate phenomenon—whether it's suicide, or sexual assault, or substance abuse, name whatever you want—anytime something like that comes up, the intuitive and first answer is always, "If we just put everybody through another training, then this would never happen again." And that's obviously not the case.

Finally, five of the military service providers we interviewed offered that it would be helpful to provide additional training for commanders that emphasizes the importance of command sensitivity to male victim needs (Table B.29).

Summary

Each victim of sexual assault is unique and will have a different constellation of needs in the days, months, and years following the assault. In this chapter, we reviewed the most common needs among male sexual assault victims, which include short-term advocacy, social support, information, mental health care, career support, and medical care. Although both male and female victims may need or benefit from similar services, the individuals we interviewed described some needs that seem to be relatively unique to male victims, including support for perceived loss of masculinity and sexual identify confusion. With the exception of military chaplains, most of the military service providers believed that members of their profession were reasonably well prepared to serve male victims. Nonetheless, most military service providers still thought that their career group would benefit from additional training about the unique reactions of male sexual assault survivors and strategies for professionally and empathetically interacting with male sexual assault victims.

CHAPTER FOUR

Reporting and Help-Seeking Among Male Sexual Assault Victims

Following a sexual assault, victims make a series of decisions about whether to disclose the assault and to whom. They may choose to reach out to informal support persons, such as friends and family, or may want or need assistance from formal support persons, such as sexual assault advocates, health care providers, and mental health counselors. Some victims may choose to involve the criminal justice system by reporting the crime or applying for a restraining order against the perpetrator. For civilians, each of these decisions can be made relatively independently. For military members, this is also true, with the exception that involving the military criminal justice system also requires involving the chain of command.

U.S. military personnel who experience a sexual assault and choose to report it may file a restricted or unrestricted report. Described in DoD Directive 6495.01 (DoD, 2012), a *restricted report* is a confidential report that allows victims to access advocate support and medical and mental health care. A restricted report is not provided to law enforcement and does not result in an investigation. The victim's command receives a notification that a sexual assault occurred but is not provided any details about the victim's or the alleged perpetrator's identity. Those who file restricted reports cannot request a military protective order or an expedited transfer because of the sexual assault.[1] Filing an *unrestricted report* allows the victim to access all the same services that a restricted report allows; in addition, filing an unrestricted report begins a criminal investigation, and the sexual assault report is disclosed to the victim's chain of command. When investigators begin interviews with the alleged perpetrator and potential witnesses, the victim's identity and the existence of an investigation become more widely known. Servicemembers who file an unrestricted report can receive a military protective order and can also request an expedited transfer to another installation.

---

[1] An *expedited transfer* is a temporary or permanent reassignment to a different installation or to a different unit within a current installation.

Likelihood of Reporting and Seeking Support

Estimates suggest that only 15 percent of military male sexual assault victims file a report (Severance, Debus, and Davis, 2017). Data published in 2017 show that, of those who did report, 31 percent filed a restricted report, 55 percent filed an unrestricted report, and 15 percent were not sure which type of report they filed (Severance, Debus, and Davis, 2017, p. 104). These findings are consistent with reporting among civilians. Although civilians can report to law enforcement without their employer being notified, the majority of civilian male sexual assault victims choose not to involve the criminal justice system (Pino and Meier, 1999).

The 2014 RMWS found that, including reporting, only 40 percent of military servicemen who were sexually assaulted had told *anyone* about the assault (Morral, Gore, and Schell, 2015a). The people whom male victims most commonly told about the assault were a friend or family member (29 percent), a supervisor or someone in their chain of command (21 percent), an officer or noncommissioned officer outside their chain of command (10 percent), or their SARC (10 percent) (Morral, Gore, and Schell, 2015a). Again, this finding appears to be consistent with male victims in the civilian population who commonly do not seek any help following an assault. Research suggests that, of civilian men who are sexually assaulted, 30 percent or less seek any kind of help (Masho and Alvanzo, 2009; Monk-Turner and Light, 2010).

Possibly because our interviewees provide a variety of services to victims, we received diverse responses when we asked what proportion of all sexual assault victims in the military report to authorities. Some interviewees provide services that tend to be connected to reporting (e.g., legal counsel), and others provide services that do not require reporting (e.g., chaplains). Overall, military service providers tended to indicate that the military sexual assault victims they have assisted had filed a report (Table B.4). Given the low rate of reporting among the population of male sexual assault victims in the military, the high rate of reporting described by service providers may indicate that their insights about male victims are not representative of the entire population and instead apply more specifically to male victims who report.

Several of the service providers we spoke with noted that, due to their professions, victims come to see them only when seeking services and are, by definition, receptive to resources. Nevertheless, the military service providers described some variability in the degree to which victims are willing to seek care from other service providers. It was common for these interviewees to indicate that they often provide referrals for services outside their specialty area. Common referrals included behavioral or mental health services, SARC or victim advocate services, medical care, legal counsel, and chaplain support (Table B.12). Most service providers who addressed referrals indicated that they have offered to connect victims to behavioral or mental health services, and a small portion of these providers specifically referenced offering off-installation behavioral health resources. Many providers indicated that they offer a standard set of services to all sexual assault victims. Legal counsel interviewees commented that they tend to interact with victims after other necessary referrals have already been provided. Military service providers were less likely to mention (1) referrals to the military's Family Advocacy Program or to law enforcement or (2) support with expedited transfers or military protective orders.

Among providers who discussed the resources they offer to male sexual assault victims in the military and compared them with the resources offered to female victims, most providers indicated that they offer similar resources to victims of either gender (Table B.13). Five indicated that they offer gender-specific treatment—for example, support groups that are open only to one gender. Of those who responded, the majority of providers indicated that most victims who were offered a referral were receptive to the referral and subsequently sought the recommended services (Table B.14).

The civilian experts we spoke with were more likely to comment that victims are not receptive to referrals. Five of the seven civilian interviewees who commented on this topic noted that men's reluctance to report an assault or access services is a key challenge to connecting them to resources. Several civilian interviewees indicated that, even among individuals seeking treatment, there may be distrust of the treatment or of other suggested resources. As one civilian mental health care provider observed,

> Some people may be very open to the services that are available and benefit from them and do well. And other people, I feel like no matter what the services are, they're still going to be angry and distrustful and might feel that they aren't getting their needs met, even if treatment that's being offered is appropriate to their concerns, because of the betrayal and distrust that they've experienced. . . . It's a range.

Gender Differences in Reporting and Help-Seeking

According to the 2016 WGRA, servicewomen who experienced a sexual assault were significantly more likely to file a report (31 percent) than servicemen were (15 percent) (Severance, Debus, and Davis, 2017). The same is true in the civilian population, where women were more likely than men to report their sexual assault to law enforcement (Pino and Meier, 1999). Servicemen were also less likely to disclose to any support person: Fewer male victims (29 percent) than female victims (56 percent) of a sexual assault in the past year had talked with a friend or family member about the assault (Morral, Gore, and Schell, 2015a).

Both the civilian experts and military service providers with whom we spoke perceived that reporting was less common among men who had been sexually assaulted relative to women (Table B.5). However, one civilian physical health care provider observed that the difference may be partially due to the likelihood of men and women being asked about victimization:

> People don't ask men whether they've been sexually assaulted, and then, of course, since they don't ask, then it doesn't get measured. And since it doesn't get measured, then we all walk around thinking that only women get sexually assaulted. But in fact, it's [that] we've only asked the women.

Furthermore, six military service providers believed that men file unrestricted reports less frequently than women (Table B.5).

When comparing help-seeking between male and female sexual assault victims, the five civilian experts who responded to this topic commented that men may be less receptive than women to following up with resources. Most military service providers who commented on this topic also believed that male victims were more reluctant than female victims to seek support and services (Table B.3) or to follow up on referrals (Table B.15). However, only a slightly smaller number of military service providers indicated that men and women are equally receptive to resources. Only three service providers indicated that men are more receptive to resources than women.

Amount of Time Victims Wait to Report

Among male and female Army soldiers who filed either an unrestricted or restricted report of sexual assault, and for whom dates on timing of the assault were available, half (50 percent) filed within one month of the assault, 31 percent waited longer than one month but less than one year to officially report the assault, and 19 percent reported the assault more than one year after it occurred (DoD, 2016b). The Defense Sexual Assault Incident Database data that are publicly released in the service branch enclosures to SAPRO annual reports do not include the detail necessary to determine whether there are gender differences in the time to report. When queried, most of the civilian experts we spoke with (six of the seven who commented) indicated that there is a wide range or too much variability across individuals to provide a reasonable estimate on gender differences in the amount of time individuals wait to report. Most military service providers who made a comparison did not perceive a difference in time to report between male and female victims (Table B.7). They did note that victims may wait to report until they are in a location that is away from their perpetrator. When commenting on trends in male sexual assault reporting, one Air Force sexual assault responder said, "Instead of being on site or on station where the individual [perpetrator] was," the victim "waited until they went [on temporary duty] or deployed and then reported because they weren't where the individual was."

Predictors of Reporting and Help-Seeking

Greater severity of sexual assault appears to be associated with greater odds that male victims will seek help. Specifically, male victims were more likely to seek help when the perpetrators used threats during the incident and when the victims believed that they were at risk of being physically injured during the incident (Masho and Alvanzo, 2009). Both men and women were more likely to report their sexual assault to police if the perpetrator was a stranger, something was stolen from them, or a weapon was present. Men, in particular, were eight times more likely to report an assault to police if they needed medical attention (Pino and Meier, 1999). Physical injury may increase the odds of male victims seeking help, but research on this association is mixed (Masho and Alvanzo, 2009; Monk-Turner and Light, 2010; Pino and Meier, 1999).

Among servicemen who experienced a sexual assault in the past year and who chose to report it, the most common motivations for reporting were to stop the offender from hurting others (45 percent) or themselves again (47 percent) or because they believed it was their civil or military duty to report (41 percent). Both men and women gave similar reasons for reporting the sexual assault to DoD, with one exception. Women (44 percent) were significantly more likely than men (22 percent) to indicate that they reported the assault because someone had encouraged them to do so (Severance, Debus, and Davis, 2017).

Among the military service providers we interviewed who commented on possible gender differences in victims' reasons for reporting, the majority indicated that they did not perceive any differences between servicemen and women or that they were unable to judge whether there were any gender differences (Table B.11).

The civilian experts we interviewed believed that victims report for a variety of reasons, including a desire to obtain justice, to prevent the perpetrator from assaulting others, and to access services. One civilian researcher described the desire for justice and the related desire to protect others from assault:

> [The victim] wants to get justice, and they don't want this person to get away with hurting them. And they also don't want them to hurt other people. There's a justice component to wanting to report and let the criminal justice system take care of the situation.

> I think the more serious the assault is in terms of injury—physical injury aside from the assault— . . . that tends to motivate people to want to report. Again, to get that person off the streets or to bring them to justice and punish them for what they did.

In addition to the motivating factors that civilian experts noted, military service provider interviewees also mentioned encouragement from others to report the assault; the assault having negative effects on the victim's life (e.g., intimate relationships); and, for some, unintentional reporting as a consequence of discussing the assault with a mandated reporter (e.g., a commander) or colleagues (Table B.10).

Of these motivators for reporting, the desire to access rights or services was discussed by the largest number of service providers. As one Marine Corps sexual assault responder noted,

> For the most part, I feel like [victims report] so they can start seeking services. The ones that do go unrestricted do tend to follow through with the law enforcement piece. . . . Getting services and medical is huge also, being able to have that forensic exam.

Service providers also mentioned seeking justice and preventing the perpetrator from assaulting others as reasons why victims report. A Navy mental health care provider commented, "Some of them have the clarity of thought where they really believe that people [who] do wrong things should be held accountable for their actions." Another Air Force mental health care provider stated,

> The most salient reason that I hear is not wanting the assailant to do the same thing to someone else. There's a pretty pervasive sense of selflessness among victims. And on some level maybe even a feeling of responsibility that, yes, this is going to be maybe a difficult and maybe a painful thing to report and to go through, but going along with the military ethos, there's this idea of being a wingman to other people. That if they don't step up and report this and have some action taken, then there could be other victims out there, and that seems to be pretty powerful for them.

Barriers to Reporting and Help-Seeking

There are several reasons that some sexual assault victims choose not to report an assault or not to seek services or support following an assault. In some cases, the victim may not be personally aware of the barriers. For example, victims who do not label the incident as a sexual assault may not be aware that this is preventing them from accessing services that could help them. In other cases, the decision whether to report is based on the victim's calculus about likely outcomes. If sexual assault victims believe that their report will not be believed or acted upon; that they will be shamed, harmed, or retaliated against for reporting; or that the system cannot protect their confidentiality, many will decide that not disclosing will protect their interests better than reporting would.

Event Not Self-Identified as a Sexual Assault

Among military servicemen who had at least one experience that can be classified as a sexual assault according to the UCMJ (see Schell et al., 2014), 26 percent indicated that the event was hazing-related (Severance, Debus, and Davis, 2017). Servicemen who are penetrated or touched on their private areas during a hazing assault are unlikely to categorize the event as "sex." Because their perpetrator(s) may not have been sexually aroused during the incident, the victims might not classify what happened to them as a "sexual assault."

A civilian mental health care provider expanded on this topic to describe other assaults that the victim may not classify as a sexual assault:

> Males tend to not even [label] what is done to them as sexual abuse, particularly if it's done in the context of hazing or any kind of sexual initiation. A lot of times, for instance, gay men who are perpetrated by older . . . men will classify that as, "Well, they taught me about sex," as opposed to they were being perpetrated. . . . The same thing with [female] teachers and males in high school. . . . A lot of them will say, "Oh, I was lucky." They don't frame it at all as sexual trauma. And society, of course, does the same thing. The sympathy goes to the female perpetrator, not to the male victim. It tends to get classified as it was a consensual relationship and that it was "a relationship." When females are sexually traumatized by a teacher, no one in society calls it a relationship. It's automatically labeled as "this is sexual trauma, period."

Two civilian experts referenced the need for men to recognize what happened to them as being sexual assault, noting that male victims may not have the same framework for such an incident as women, because men are not socialized to have such a framework. One researcher commented,

> For men, they don't grow up with the idea that someday they may be sexually assaulted. . . . They don't have a framework for evaluating what has happened to them and understanding that something very bad has happened to them and that a violation has indeed occurred. And so, they are kind of in limbo as to coming to terms with what happened to them.

Belief That Nothing Will Be Done

Victims who identify their experience as a sexual assault consider what they know about their social and professional context and make predictions about the outcomes associated with disclosing their victimization experience. Many predict that they will not be believed (Turchik, McLean, et al., 2013) or that nothing will be done in response. Among male sexual assault victims in the military who chose not to report the assault, 29 percent indicated that at least one of their reasons was that "they didn't think anything would be done" (Severance, Debus, and Davis, 2017). Thirty percent did not believe the process would be fair (Severance, Debus, and Davis, 2017). If the perpetrator is a high performer or leader, victims may believe that the charges will simply be dismissed (Castro et al., 2015). A civilian researcher we interviewed told us that victims' beliefs that nothing would be done are expression of their lack of confidence in the system. The military service providers we interviewed reiterated this lack of confidence in the system and the common fear among male victims that they will not be believed even if they do come forward. A Navy mental health care provider noted,

> For men, I don't think they even think they'll be believed. . . . If they're gay, they think that, "oh, everyone is going to think it was consensual." And then if they're straight, then they think, "oh, everyone is going to think that really I'm gay, and I really wanted it." . . . Whether they're gay or straight, it doesn't seem to matter. They both feel like they're somehow going to be judged to be participants in it and willing participants in it.

Expectations of Negative Consequences for Disclosure

Many sexual assault victims choose not to report their assault or not to seek advocacy, medical care, or mental health care services because they believe that there will be negative consequences for doing so. This perception might be an accurate reflection of the possible outcomes of reporting: Of military sexual assault victims who reported the assault, 42 percent of men and 28 percent of women experienced reprisal, ostracism, or maltreatment as a consequence (Severance, Debus, and Davis, 2017). Perhaps because they had observed or understood this reality, many male victims of military sexual assaults indicated that they chose not to report because they were worried about negative consequences from the perpetrator(s) (21 percent), their supervisor or chain of command (26 percent), or military coworkers and peers (30 percent) (Severance, Debus, and Davis, 2017). In our interviews, civilian experts and military service providers both frequently mentioned fear of retaliation as a common barrier to reporting (Table B.8).

Victims may also worry that they will be treated poorly by criminal justice, medical, or mental health professionals. There may be a grain of truth to this perception. The published literature suggests that many civilian police officers are not prepared to assist male sexual assault victims and may hold negative attitudes toward male victims (Javaid, 2014, 2017). Medical students view male sexual assault victims more negatively than female victims (Anderson and Quinn, 2009). In addition, qualitative research with male civilian victims reveals that some have negative experiences with service providers, including dismissive treatment from social workers and counselors, insensitivity from police, and poor treatment by medical professionals (Washington, 1999). Among servicemembers who reported a sexual assault, servicemen were significantly less likely than servicewomen to be satisfied with the response and services they received from their unit commander, SARC, special victims' counsel, and chaplain (Severance, Debus, and Davis, 2017). There were no significant gender differences in satisfaction with care from medical care providers, mental health care providers, and law enforcement (Severance, Debus, and Davis, 2017). As a result, some male victims may approach service providers for help with the symptoms or consequences following an assault but decline to provide information about the assault itself (O'Brien, Keith, and Shoemaker, 2015; Turchik and Edwards, 2012). After interviewing U.S. veterans, researchers found that concern about the sensitivity of providers was a barrier to seeking MST-related services (Turchik, McLean, et al., 2013).

Finally, many victims, both men and women, are concerned about the negative repercussions that being a victim could have on their career. A civilian mental health care provider noted,

> Many survivors are afraid that they'll be stigmatized, particularly when you talk about people in the military, or anybody who's now an adult who has any kind of position like working with kids or a position of authority. I mean, the fears are tremendous that . . . "No one will trust me. No one will trust me around children." That there's some kind of belief that this makes them mentally ill.

Military service providers mentioned concerns about possible disciplinary actions for collateral misconduct (e.g., underage drinking prior to the assault) as a barrier and emphasized worry about how reporting sexual assaults could affect military careers (Table B.8). This was mentioned as a barrier for victims of both genders, but four providers believed that servicewomen had more concerns than servicemen did about career harm (Table B.9). Indeed, the perceived gender difference is borne out by survey data from military sexual assault victims. According to the 2016 WGRA, servicewomen (36 percent) were significantly more likely than servicemen (24 percent) to indicate that one of their reasons for not reporting the sexual assault was that they thought it might hurt their career (Severance, Debus, and Davis, 2017).

As one Navy legal counselor commented,

> There is still this concern or stigma in the military that if you seek medical assistance, it's going to somehow get you on the track out of the Navy. I see that with all of my victims, men or women—just that they're always a little bit hesitant about, "Okay, if I go see this doctor, it's going to mean I'm going to get kicked out."

Similarly, a Marine Corps mental health care provider noted,

> For an active-duty military, they're more resistant to getting medical needs because it's going to go in their record and it's going to follow them. And then the fear is that it will somehow impact their career, their tenure, the ability to promote.

Shame, Embarrassment, and Loss of Masculinity

Among U.S. servicemen, stereotypes about masculinity, including views of men as sexually assertive and powerful, and men's beliefs in male sexual assault myths may hinder reporting and help-seeking among victims (Castro et al., 2015; Morris et al., 2014). U.S. military men can feel humiliated following a sexual assault, particularly if they had previously believed that men cannot be raped. In interviews with veterans who had experienced MST, many cited embarrassment and shame as barriers to help-seeking among male veterans (Turchik, McLean, et al., 2013). This shame may be reflected in the reasons that sexually assaulted servicemen give for not filing an official report. More than one-third indicated that they did not want to feel shamed or embarrassed (37 percent) or be perceived as weak (44 percent) (Severance, Debus, and Davis, 2017).

The civilian experts we interviewed also cited shame and self-blame as common barriers to reporting among both male and female sexual assault victims. Commenting on both men and women, a mental health care provider noted,

> In general, shame is the biggest block to anybody coming forward. They're so embarrassed by it. Because . . . most survivors tend to take some responsibility for being perpetrated, for being violated. They somehow believe that they must have had something to do with it. And, of course, perpetrators do everything in their power to make sure that the victim believes that. So, shame is huge and the lack of understanding that they have zero responsibility for it. Many survivors are afraid that they won't be believed, or that they'll be punished, or that they'll be shamed because people/society will also blame them.

Although experts saw shame as a barrier to reporting and help-seeking for both men and women, six of the eight civilian experts indicated that shame and self-blame are more prevalent among male sexual assault victims than among female victims. One mental health care provider explained,

> I think that society is a little more accepting of women coming forward and being victims. It's much more recognized that women get sexually abused. It is much less recognized that males get abused too. It's especially less recognized that males can be abused by females. That's the biggest block—that is, if a man was abused by a female . . . it's so difficult to come forward, because there's so much embarrassment that "I should've been in control, and I wasn't. I should've been able to stop it, and I didn't." . . . Male socialization is all about teaching them that we're supposed to be powerful and strong. And if you're a victim of sexual trauma, then a man or a boy tends to believe that he's weak and powerless, and there's something wrong with him. And generally, women don't think that. They do to some degree, of course, because, unfortunately, the same kind of stigma exists. But I think society is much more willing to help women understand it's not their fault, whereas men tend not to believe that.

The military service providers we interviewed held similar perspectives. They noted that military victims' self-blame, embarrassment, and shame are significant barriers to reporting and connecting them to services (Table B.8), and, like the civilian experts, the military service providers identified embarrassment as a particularly potent barrier for male victims (Table B.9). As one Navy physical health care provider commented,

> Women, they don't want to be blamed because of maybe the way they dressed or the fact [that people] might look at them [and think], "Well, if you weren't out by yourself," that kind of thing. Men don't want to be looked at as weak or non-masculine, that type of thing. So, stigma plays a major role in both male and female reporting.

Most providers who perceived gender differences described this shame as more prominent in military male victims than in military female victims and highlighted the men's perceived loss of masculinity. For example, one mental health care provider for the Navy indicated that male victims are "going to think somehow that 'I'm tainted in some way' or that 'I'm not going to be like a real man anymore.' . . . The shame is just intensified, I think." An Army physical health care provider told us,

> I think it's probably a lot harder for a male to come forward than a female to come forward. Because a male, in all the training that I've received, they associate it with weakness. Well, the stigma that is associated with the feelings they might have: "Am I gay? Am I weak? Is this my fault?" . . . I think that men just have just a harder time processing this than the females do.

Similarly, an Army chaplain told us, "I would say my gentlemen have been more concerned with unrestricted reports because there's more stigma and they may not want people to know and they have been sort of more mortified."

While military service providers noted the role that shame plays in potentially preventing male victims from filing a restricted or an unrestricted report, they also saw shame as a barrier to help-seeking. Service providers indicated that they sometimes struggled to connect servicemen who had experienced a sexual assault to services. Commenting on this, an Army sexual assault responder stated, "I think that offering services to men comes with shame, and it somehow takes a little bit away from who they think they are, and especially behavioral health [services]." Discussing the challenge of convincing male victims to seek specialized care, a Navy chaplain offered a metaphor used with male victims:

> It's getting them past the perception that this is for women and that [resources] are there to support you as well, and to try to add perspective to the shame that they feel and to try to explain how they might benefit from those resources that will help them. . . . Sometimes I put it in layman terms that, look, I'm a country doctor, a family doctor, and you need to see a brain surgeon. You wouldn't want your general practitioner doing open heart surgery, because there are specialists for that, and what you're talking about, you really need to have a specialist because . . . it was a damaging thing that was done to you.

Protecting One's Privacy

Evidence suggests that barriers to reporting and help-seeking, for both veterans and active-duty servicemembers, include the desire to maintain one's privacy and a lack of confidence in the confidentiality of medical, mental health, or other services (Turchik, McLean, et al., 2013). Among military male sexual assault victims who chose not to report, 39 percent cited "did not want more people to know" as one reason, and 25 percent cited "did not think [their] report would be kept confidential" (Severance, Debus, and Davis, 2017).

Privacy concerns were cited as a common barrier to reporting and help-seeking by the military service providers we interviewed (Table B.8). However, only four providers believed that this was a more potent barrier for men than for women (Table B.9). This is a perception that is supported by the most recent WGRA data, which showed that servicewomen who did not report a sexual assault were significantly more likely than men to cite "did not want more people to know" as a reason (Severance, Debus, and Davis, 2017). Servicemen and women did not have significantly different concerns about the confidentiality of their report (Severance, Debus, and Davis, 2017).

When military victims are motivated to protect their privacy, accessing DoD services on base may be perceived as a risky choice. The victims may worry that their discussions with service providers will not be kept confidential, or they may fear that military colleagues will see them entering or in the waiting area of a SARC office or mental health care facility. We asked the military service providers we interviewed whether they believed that male and female sexual assault victims have concerns about accessing DoD or military services, and most providers who responded to this question did not believe that this was a significant concern (Table B.16).[2] Sixteen of the providers who commented, however, perceived that sexual assault victims may have such concerns. When providers discussed potential reasons for concerns about accessing DoD or military services, three primary themes arose (Table B.17). The most commonly discussed theme was that sexual assault victims are concerned about maintaining privacy and confidentiality when accessing DoD or military services. A Marine Corps physical health care provider explained,

> Especially when you're at a very small command where we have all these resources available to them, there is a perception that "People are going to see me going there. People are going to see me going to behavioral health and they're going to know I'm in there, and they're going to know why." . . . If we could guarantee that nobody is going to see them walk into behavioral health and wonder why they walk in there, it would be so much easier. But the problem is that I am at this small command. When they walk into behavioral health, they could be seen by a bunch of other people within their unit, and they're like, "Well, what are you going there for?"

---

[2]   However, because military providers see only victims who have chosen to access DoD services, the may not have good visibility into victims who prefer not to use DoD services.

A Navy chaplain also noted victims' worry about accessing DoD services but did not perceive off-installation services as necessarily the best answer either:

> Now, often . . . they'll say . . . "I really don't want to engage the military community, because it's just too close to home for me." So, I'll also share some resources that are . . . within the municipalities that they can access. But a lot of males don't feel comfortable with that because . . . resources in most of our municipalities are geared towards women and not towards men. And so, it makes them feel even more isolated.

Concern About One's Unit

Finally, some researchers have proposed that low rates of male sexual assault reporting in the U.S. military may be related to a perceived code of silence regarding these experiences and concern that reporting may be seen as betraying one's unit, particularly if the perpetrator or perpetrators are part of the unit (Castro et al., 2015). It is also notable that sexual assault is one of the few events that is exempt from military guidance to resolve conflict "at the lowest possible level." For example, even service members who are sexually harassed are encouraged to resolve the conflict directly or as low in their own military chain of command as possible. In a culture that trains individuals to prioritize direct conflict resolution, it may be psychologically difficult for male sexual assault victims to elevate their complaint even though they are allowed by policy to do so. The military service providers we spoke with did not mention military or unit commitment as a perceived barrier to reporting and help-seeking among the male victims they had served. Concern about harming one's unit is not included in the WGRA as a survey item.

Strategies to Improve Reporting and Help-Seeking

Belief in myths about male sexual assault may hinder male victims' reporting and help-seeking (Turchik, Pavao, Nazarian, et al., 2012). Thus, one avenue for promoting help-seeking among male servicemembers who have experienced sexual assault is to dispel myths that those in the U.S. military community may believe regarding male sexual assault. To do so, researchers suggest including examples of male sexual assault survivors in educational materials (O'Brien, Keith, and Shoemaker, 2015). These materials should also include accurate information about sexual assault against men and women to begin to replace the inaccurate myths that some servicemembers may believe (Turchik and Edwards, 2012).

The armed services provide annual SAPR training to servicemembers, and some research suggests that the training increases knowledge of available support services and protocols (Holland, Rabelo, and Cortina, 2014). However, SAPR training may focus on female sexual assault victims and male perpetrators. To consider the influence of gender preferences in SAPR materials provided to servicemembers, research has assessed the influence of gender-neutral sexual assault training on perceptions among U.S. Naval Academy midshipmen (Rosenstein, 2015). In this gender-neutral training, gender and sex were not referenced in presented slides, and discussion points emphasized gender equivalence, noting that male or female perpetrators could assault male or female victims. Participation in at least one gender-neutral training was associated with lower acceptance of male and female sexual assault myths among both male and female midshipmen.

Utilization of gender-inclusive, rather than simply gender-neutral, training may also be worthwhile to further reduce belief in male and female sexual assault myths (Rosenstein, 2015). Gender-inclusive training would include explicit discussion of male sexual assault victims. Research has shown that male veterans prefer to obtain gender-targeted information regarding sexual assault (i.e., men who have experienced MST prefer to receive information on male victims), rather than gender-neutral information (Turchik, Rafie, et al., 2014). However, it is not yet clear whether these gender-targeted materials promote greater help-seeking among victims.

When men approach service providers and have indicators suggestive of sexual victimization, researchers suggest that service providers reference the experiences of male sexual assault victims in general and provide information regarding support for male sexual assault victims (Polusny and Murdoch, 2005). Providing this information may help to combat victim perceptions that sexual assault does not happen to men. In addition, instituting routine questions regarding sexual assault experiences for both male and female servicemembers seeking certain mental, medical, or other support services may also encourage servicemembers to disclose their sexual assault experiences (Polusny and Murdoch, 2005).

When the military provides training and educational materials that consider male sexual assault victims, male servicemembers who experience sexual assault may not only be more willing to seek help following an assault but may also be more willing to report their assault through official channels (O'Brien, Keith, and Shoemaker, 2015; Scarce, 1997; Turchik and Edwards, 2012). However, if victims perceive that those to whom they report will react negatively or with disbelief, the victims may be unlikely to report being sexually assaulted. To promote reporting, male sexual assault victims must know that the professionals to whom they disclose will not express negative attitudes toward them or disbelief in their account of the assault (Javaid, 2017).

Six of eight civilian experts we interviewed also commented on ways in which service settings should be made more welcoming of male victims or ways in which service providers should be specially trained on male victim needs, echoing the published suggestions described earlier. One civilian mental health care provider emphasized that all staff—not only treatment providers but also administrative staff who arrange appointments—should be trained to be sensitive to male victims. A civilian researcher elaborated on this point, saying,

> I think the paradigm usually is that men are the offenders and women are the victims. And so I think that men have never felt welcomed to call hotlines or to walk into a rape crisis center. So, somehow things would have to change a bit to make it more welcoming for them, so that they wouldn't feel like people would be a little bit more skeptical of their being there at all.

A civilian mental health care provider commented on supporting client receptivity while making referrals, stating,

> I think once people get to me, if I can assure them that wherever I'm referring them to—like if somebody were sexually assaulted and came to me—I would feel comfortable saying there's a specific division in the [city] police department that handles these kinds of things and I can assure you that they're safe people to talk to. So it has to be that I can assure them of that.

Finally, the resources may not need to be different, just welcoming, as another civilian mental health care provider noted:

> I don't think the resources need to be different. What needs to be different is that there's an awareness that men are safe there too. I've talked to the military about the . . . quote that "one of a hundred men in the military gets sexually abused." And I said, "Really? Think about it. If you're one out of the hundred, how likely is it you're going to come forward if you think 'I'm the one that was the weakling. I'm the one who didn't fight back'?"

Military service providers offered similar comments but also emphasized the need to protect the privacy of male victims. A Marine Corps chaplain stated,

> Men, just because of that factor of what it does to them as men and the way they see themselves—"I'll handle my own problem"—they tend to not report. And so, I'd just go back with they need, more than anything else, someplace that they can go to where they can be anonymous. They need to know what the resources are if they want to take advantage of it, but they also need to know what the resources are outside the institutional organization so that if they won't use the institution for help and the program that's there, that they can go get some sort of private help on the outside.

Summary

Previous research suggests that most military male sexual assault victims choose not to file a restricted or an unrestricted report, and many do not seek support services. These choices are influenced by the victims not labeling the incident as "sexual assault" and the beliefs that their report will not be believed or acted upon; that they will be shamed, harmed, or retaliated against for reporting; or that the system cannot protect their confidentiality. For the minority of male victims who do report their assault, motivators include an acute need for services (e.g., to treat injuries), to prevent the offender(s) from hurting others, to obtain justice, and to fulfill their civil or military duty. To encourage reporting and help-seeking among servicemen who have been sexually assaulted, SAPR training should continue to address male sexual assault and include portrayals of male victims, and services and service providers must be welcoming to male victims, treat them with respect, and protect their privacy.

CHAPTER FIVE

Improving Knowledge and Correcting Misperceptions About Male Sexual Assault

Much of the research on male sexual assault has considered public perceptions of such assault, including false and prejudicial beliefs, and the potential impact of these perceptions on male victims (Davies and Rogers, 2006; Light and Monk-Turner, 2009). In this chapter, we review research describing public perceptions of male sexual assault, as well as the public outreach campaigns designed to correct misconceptions. Throughout, we draw on the published literature on military perception of male sexual assault where available, but we also rely heavily on the expertise of the civilian experts and DoD service providers we interviewed to fill gaps in the research literature.

How Male Sexual Assault Victims Are Perceived

Among all sexual assault victims serving in the military, approximately half are men (Morral, Gore, and Schell, 2015b). Nonetheless, male sexual assault victims continue to be underrecognized and underserved for a variety of reasons (Castro et al., 2015; Turchik and Edwards, 2012). During our interviews, we asked civilian experts and military service providers their thoughts about how the general population and general military population perceived male victims of sexual assault. We were interested in documenting the extent to which perceptions of male victims matched the empirical evidence about their experiences (reviewed in Chapter Two).

Among military service providers, opinions were mixed about whether the general military population had an adequate understanding that men can be victims of sexual assault (Table B.19). Although male sexual assault is addressed in military sexual assault prevention training, some military providers believed that servicemembers maintain their stereotypes regarding male sexual assault even after receiving this training. One Marine Corps legal counselor commented,

> I don't know if the average servicemember believes that it really happens. And of course, they've heard people talk about it and we now have DoD SAPR training that includes vignettes with male victims. So, they know that it's discussed, but I don't really see a groundswell of understanding that it's a problem. Because the

cases that I've seen still—command members still treat them with a wary glance. Like, "Oh, really? Is this really a legit thing? Or is this just [the] kind of a problem that we have because we've appealed [to] that? What exactly are we dealing with here, there, legal guy? Explain this to me."

Comparing servicemember knowledge about male and female sexual assault, providers perceived that servicemembers either know less about male sexual assault than about female sexual assault or know an equal amount about both (Table B.20). Commenting on how servicemembers may know less about male than female sexual assault, an Army service provider stated,

> When you talk about sexual assault against [a] female, I think people know all kinds of things; like alcohol is typically involved, that most victims are women, most perpetrators are men. I think they know all kinds of statistics. I think they know things like, "no means no." So, there's been a lot of effort into those narratives, but we really haven't talked much about the male side of things. What are the factors involved? Who are the perpetrators of male sexual assault? What kind of situational factors are present? I don't think we ever talk about that stuff.[1]

In our discussions with research experts on civilian sexual assault, all of the experts who offered a comparison of the general public's understanding of male sexual assault (six) agreed that the public has greater knowledge or understanding of sexual assaults against women than of those perpetrated against men. One expert stated, "I really don't think too many people know, and, honestly, there hasn't really been that much concern about [sexual assaults against men]." A civilian researcher noted,

> There's just so many stereotypes involved with all of this stuff and particularly for men just in the idea that . . . real men, if you start getting into the nitty-gritty of the definition of masculinity, that they're not supposed to be victims. And that this is a crime that's been constructed in everybody's mindset as a woman's crime.

Male Rape Myths

Reduced reporting among men, as well as limited public understanding, may keep the population of male victims more hidden than the population of female victims. The lack of public exposure to men who have survived a sexual assault may explain, in part, some individuals' acceptance of myths about sexual assault against men. *Sexual assault myths*, also known as *rape myths*, include false beliefs about sexual assault and beliefs that hold victims responsible for the assault while justifying the actions of the perpetrator (Chapleau, Oswald, and Russell, 2008). In our review of the literature

---

[1]   Per this interviewee's request, we do not state the interviewee's occupation.

(Sivakumaran, 2005; Struckman-Johnson, 1988; Turchik and Edwards, 2012), some commonly held myths regarding male sexual assault include the following:

- Men cannot be sexually assaulted.
- Men who are sexually assaulted are to blame for not being more careful.
- Men who are sexually assaulted are to blame for not escaping from or fighting off their perpetrator.
- Men who are sexually assaulted do not need counseling after the incident.
- Only gay men, not heterosexual men, can be sexual assault victims.
- Only gay men, not heterosexual men, assault male victims.
- Women cannot sexually assault men.
- Men are sexually assaulted only in prison.
- Same-sex sexual assaults cause victims to become gay.
- Victim erection or ejaculation indicates consent.

For civilians, one of the most widely believed sexual assault myths, by both men and women, is that men who are sexually assaulted are partially to blame for not escaping or fighting off their perpetrator (Chapleau, Oswald, and Russell, 2008; Turchik and Edwards, 2012). When male victims who are presumed to be heterosexual are assaulted by a woman, some civilians believe that the victims were more likely to have encouraged or enjoyed the assault and that they experienced less stress following the assault relative to female victims of sexual assault (Smith, Pine, and Hawley, 1988). The legacy of past legal civilian codes that excluded men from definitions of sexual assault victims continues to be reflected in the perception of sexual assault by those in the general population. In the United States, one dominant sexual victimization paradigm is that men are sexual assault perpetrators and women are sexual assault victims (Stemple and Meyer, 2014). This paradigm can lead to disbelief and skepticism toward male victims, particularly if they were victimized by a woman (Sivakumaran, 2005; Struckman-Johnson, 1988; Turchik and Edwards, 2012).

In our interviews with civilian experts and military service providers, we heard this research echoed in their own experiences with victims or victim research. As one civilian researcher explained,

> If a man claims that a woman assaulted him . . . there's a lot of disbelief that that could've even happened: "How can a woman overpower a man?" or "Why wouldn't he like it if she did?" And so, there's just this assumption that (a) Men always want sex, so what's the problem? Why should he care? or (b) there's something wrong with him that even allowed an assault to have happened. And if the offender is a man, then you get into issues where there are still homophobic . . . responses if he's not gay, and if he is gay and he doesn't want people to know, that could be a problem.

As this expert alluded to, some individuals believe that gay men who are sexually assaulted by a male perpetrator hold more responsibility for the assault and experience less-severe trauma following the assault than heterosexual men who are sexually assaulted by a male perpetrator; some also believe that gay men might derive pleasure from being assaulted (Doherty and Anderson, 2004; Mitchell, Hirschman, and Nagayama Hall, 1999).

Participants in civilian research are more likely to blame male victims for being sexually assaulted when they do not fight back, do not resist, or appear scared or when the perpetrator is an acquaintance of the victim (Davies and Rogers, 2006; Sleath and Bull, 2010). Sleath and Bull (2010) notes that these findings are consistent with the research on victim-blaming against female victims. Overall, relative to women, men are less sympathetic toward victims and hold victims more accountable for the assault (Davies and Rogers, 2006; Davies, Gilston, and Rogers, 2012). In addition, people who are older, less educated, and have negative attitudes toward gay men show more support for sexual assault myths (Davies, Gilston, and Rogers, 2012; Kassing, Beesley, and Frey, 2005).

When we asked military service providers about the general military population's perception of male victims, providers described several misperceptions that echoed those described in the civilian literature, including the following:

- Men cannot be sexually assaulted.
- Male victims are to blame for being sexually assaulted.
- Male victims are weak.
- Only gay men can be victims.
- Only gay men are perpetrators.
- Male sexual assault is funny.

The fact that servicemen who identify as gay, bisexual, or transgender are more vulnerable to sexual assault may contribute to the public misconception that most or all male victims are gay (Davis, Vega, and McLeod, 2017). It is a common innumeracy to assume that if a group is at higher risk than another, then they necessarily make up a large proportion of those who experience the risk (see Villejoubert and Mandel, 2002, for review), which is usually not true unless both groups are similar in size.

Unique to the themes described by military service providers (relative to the civilian literature), and also the most commonly mentioned theme (Table B.21), was that sexual assaults against men are funny. One Army sexual assault responder offered the following description:

> A perfect example: They're out at a party. They're drinking. Somebody's like, "Oh hey, this is going to be funny. Let me tea bag [press my testicles on] this guy." They don't realize that that is not a joke. . . . They don't seem to comprehend quite as well as a female that anything involving particular body parts or doing something to another person can actually be a sexual assault versus "hey, this is funny."

Another great example is the stupid nut-tap game they're always doing. . . . They'll walk by each other and backhand each other in the nuts. And everybody's like, "ha ha, funny," because the guy is on the ground in pain or whatever. But they don't realize that's aggravated sexual contact. I think it's more difficult for them to differentiate between what they consider typical male behavior and actual sexual assault.

Another provider, a legal counselor with the Marine Corps, touched on this theme in the context of hazing assaults:

There's a lot of hazing-type things that go on, indoctrination-type things that happen. And a lot of times those things meet the legal elements of sexual assault, but those men don't think of themselves as a victim of sexual assault. . . . So, I think there's still probably an attitude [that's] dismissive of it. . . . Just Marines horsing around and they take it too far.

To the extent that male sexual assault victims are aware of culturally shared beliefs that discredit victims, they may understand that they will not be believed or will be blamed for the assault (in different ways) whether their perpetrator was a man or woman. Men who believe sexual assault myths and are subsequently victimized may have particular difficulty after their assault. In a study of U.S. veterans, higher rape myth acceptance among victims was associated with decreased self-efficacy and increased psychiatric symptoms (Voller et al., 2015). Additional research on sexual assault myth acceptance among U.S. military samples, particularly those who have and have not experienced sexual assault, is needed to better understand the potential impact on coping among male victims.

Perceptions of Campaigns to Educate Servicemembers About Male Sexual Assault

Given evidence that servicemembers may not recognize that male sexual assault can occur and may have other misconceptions about such assaults, it seems clear that efforts to improve servicemembers' understanding are needed. In the published literature, researchers have advocated for education that would dispel myths about sexual assault against men (Turchik and Edwards, 2012) and have encouraged inclusion of examples of male sexual assault survivors in educational materials (O'Brien, Keith, and Shoemaker, 2015). The U.S. military services provide annual SAPR training to all servicemembers (see, for example, DoD, 2013), and it appears to increase knowledge of available support services and protocols (Holland, Rabelo, and Cortina, 2014). In the past, these annual trainings focused heavily on female sexual assault victims and male perpetrators, but they now include male-specific sexual assault scenarios, and DoD is working to develop "learning objectives to improve Servicemembers' understanding of male sexual assault" (DoD, 2016b, p. 11).

Rosenstein (2015) showed that U.S. Naval Academy midshipmen who were exposed to introductory SAPR trainings that used gender-neutral language shifted toward lower endorsement of male sexual assault myths following the training.[2] The evaluation did not contrast the training with gender-inclusive training (e.g., training that includes examples of male victims or provides education specifically about male sexual assault), and Rosenstein (2015) suggests that doing so would be useful to determine whether gender-inclusive training might have an added benefit. Indeed, the DoD *Plan to Prevent and Respond to Sexual Assault of Military Men* specifically states,

> The creation and issuance of gender-neutral communication materials alone is not sufficient. Sexual assault victimization is so strongly associated with women that gender-neutral materials often do not resonate with men. Communication materials must directly acknowledge the broad experiences of males who experience sexual assault and bolster their confidence in the reporting process. (DoD, 2016b, p. 12)

Other research has shown that male veterans prefer to receive gender-targeted sexual assault materials (e.g., a brochure designed specifically for male victims of MST) rather than gender-neutral information (e.g., a brochure that does not reference the gender of MST victims) (Turchik, Rafie, et al., 2014). However, it is not yet clear whether these gender-targeted materials successfully increase help-seeking among male victims.

Although the military sexual assault prevention trainings that are delivered to all servicemembers are the primary vehicle by which information is disseminated to both victims and the general military population, the military services have also supported other outreach activities to increase the public's awareness of and empathy toward sexual assault victims. When we asked the military service providers we interviewed whether they were aware of outreach campaigns, most referenced annual trainings from the SAPR or Sexual Harassment/Assault Response and Prevention programs or the Sexual Assault Awareness and Prevention Month activities that are sponsored by these programs. Beyond these efforts, service providers also mentioned

- 1in6.org
- A Voice Unheard Is an Army Defeated
- Alcohol De-Glamorization
- Bystander Intervention (e.g., Green Dot)
- Clothesline Project

---

[2] The gender-neutral materials avoided referencing gender in the presented slides, and discussion points noted that a man or woman could sexually assault either a man or woman.

- DenimDayUSA.org
- I.A.M. Strong
- National Sexual Assault Conference
- No Means No
- Not on My Team
- Protecting Our People Protects Our Mission
- Texas Association Against Sexual Assault
- Walk in Her Shoes.

Notably, several of these outreach efforts are not administered by military offices responsible for SAPR or by the military more broadly, and several of these efforts are not specifically targeted to military personnel.

We asked whether any outreach efforts addressed male sexual victims specifically, and of the interviewees who commented on this, the most frequently discussed theme was that the campaigns were designed to address sexual assault more broadly, without a focus on either male or female victims (Table B.22). Several interviewees indicated that male sexual assault was not specifically addressed in the outreach campaigns that they had been exposed to. An Army sexual assault responder offered, "I think that's an area the DoD needs some improvement on—getting the male-on-male message out there more. Because even now when I teach classes, . . . people have a tendency to equate sexual assault with a male-on-female situation." Six interviewees indicated awareness of outreach campaigns that specifically focused on male sexual assault (Table B.22).

In our interviews, we queried the perceived efficacy of outreach efforts.[3] The largest number of service providers who responded to this question indicated that they believed that the outreach campaigns were effective (Table B.23). Expanding on why they perceived these efforts to be effective, service providers often noted that they believed that the campaigns had promoted sexual assault awareness or sexual assault reporting in the military population. One Marine Corps sexual assault responder commented,

> When I talk to Marines and sailors, they're tired of getting SAPR briefs, because we give them so much. "Oh, we know sexual assault. We know. We know. We know." But the reality is, for those people who say they know, there's a lot of people who don't know. It's always a privilege to get out and talk about the program—give information out—because every time you go out and do [a] training, there's somebody who didn't know it. Because they'll come up and tell you, "Oh, I didn't know we could do that!" or "I didn't know that resource was available on installation." The more we get out, the better.

---

[3] We did not provide a definition of *efficacy*. Rather, we encouraged service providers to comment based on their own conceptualizations.

However, the opinion that outreach efforts are effective was not universal, and some interviewees indicated that they perceived the campaigns as only somewhat effective or were not certain how effective the campaigns were. Four providers indicated that the campaigns were not at all effective. Interviewees tended to discuss general perceptions of efficacy or provide anecdotal evidence regarding efficacy. They did not discuss systematic evaluations of any campaigns.

Interviewees' Suggestions on How to Improve Education Campaigns Addressing Male Sexual Assault

The civilian experts we interviewed provided a range of recommendations for improving sexual assault outreach campaigns. Two of the six civilian experts who commented on this topic noted that there are lessons to be learned from successful safety and public health campaigns that have shifted societal norms (e.g., seatbelt use, breastfeeding). Other recommendations included the following:

- Address sexual harassment alongside sexual assault.
- Conduct research to better understand the problem.
- Implement campaigns more often and more visibly.
- Increase demographic diversity represented in campaigns.
- Incorporate both male and female victims as a focus in campaigns.
- Address myths about male victims.

Describing the need for increased demographic diversity, one civilian mental health care provider stated,

> [Campaigns] need to show diverse survivors so that it's not just white survivors, but African Americans, and Latino, and transgender, gay, and bisexual [survivors]. And . . . that's what will be effective in helping people know that anybody can be sexually abused. . . . That's what I think is effective.

Discussing the recommendations that messaging should address myths about male victims and that research support is necessary, one interviewee described the potential value of aligning conceptions of masculinity with the courage required to come forward as a survivor. As noted earlier, some members of the public believe that male victims are weak, and this civilian mental health care provider noted that it will be important to look at

> research that evaluates how you actually debunk some of the myths about male rape effectively. I think another related . . . but still very important area is just research on masculinity and how that impacts male survivors' responses to sexual

assault. . . . What kinds of campaigns or messages, or even treatments, can help men reclaim their masculinity or define a healthy masculinity for themselves? For example, to realize that it's not weak to ask for help but, in fact, it takes a lot of bravery and strength to do that. . . . I think it needs to be much more researched and better understood first, and then absolutely needs to make it into trainings and campaigns and practices after that.

The military service providers we interviewed heavily emphasized the importance of using engaging materials and presentations and specifically suggested avoiding PowerPoint presentations that do not promote audience engagement. They believed that servicemembers learn very little during these presentations.

With respect to educating the military public about male sexual assault in particular, military service providers suggested several options (Table B.24). For example, they recommended providing servicemembers with specific information about the characteristics of male sexual assault. One Navy mental health care provider expanded on this suggestion, saying,

I always think that the results of [male sexual assault] cases need to be made public. . . . I think that helps a lot when people can see the consequences of cases. You don't even have to include names, but you can say a male perpetrator and a male victim and this is what happened. Those are the things . . . that help people realize that the program is working when they see that there are consequences. And especially with males when they see, yes, these things do happen but look at what happened to the people that [committed the assault]. Look at the consequences they got. The military is on top of it. They are working, and they are punishing people who are doing these things. That helps to make people more comfortable coming forward.

In addition, three service providers recommended developing outreach material that specifically addresses male sexual assault. For example, a Navy physical health care provider commented on the need to include "some of the real [male sexual assault] stories that are out there. . . . This is 2017, and there are still things that we're afraid to talk about, which is unbelievable." Providers also recommended including content that would correct misconceptions about male sexual assault victims. Other topics that service providers suggested addressing in the context of male sexual assault included masculinity and male identity, the potential influence of alcohol misuse, and the importance of addressing related unprofessional behaviors (e.g., sexual harassment, hazing). Some providers also recommended holding small group sessions with male servicemembers, which they believed might better promote open discussion.

Although not noted by interviewees, we note the previously reviewed research that shows that, for military men, many sexual assaults occur as part of hazing incidents (Severance, Debus, and Davis, 2017). Researchers in the published literature have suggested that male-focused sexual assault prevention efforts specifically address the lack of tolerance for hazing and hazing-related sexual assaults (Scarce, 1997). Promoting leadership engagement, including lack of tolerance for misconduct, may also assist with reducing hazing and male sexual assaults that may occur during these activities (Keller, Matthews, and Hall, 2015).

Summary

In this chapter, we summarized public misconceptions of male sexual assaults, which sometimes fail to acknowledge that male victims exist, blame victims for being weak or "letting" the assault happen, and assume a stereotypical assailant. In some cases, these misperceptions are based on a kernel of truth. For example, the substantially increased risk for sexual assault among gay servicemen is misinterpreted by some individuals to mean that all male victims are gay. Other misperceptions seem to arise from shared cultural norms, such as the belief that sexual contact crimes that men perpetrate against other men are funny jokes as opposed to criminal actions. Given these misperceptions (and for other reasons), the military service branches have implemented annual SAPR trainings, as well as other outreach activities, to improve understanding of military sexual assaults and to try to mitigate common sexual assault myths. The civilian experts and military service providers we interviewed shared several recommendations to improve these outreach activities. Civilian experts recommended that the military draw insight from the lessons learned from successful public outreach campaigns related to public health. Military service providers recommended that any outreach activities use engaging formats, provide information that counters male sexual assault myths, and include portrayals of male sexual assault survivors.

CHAPTER SIX

Recommendations

Information from previous research and our interviews with experts and service providers suggest several potential avenues for DoD to consider as part of its efforts to improve response to sexual assaults against men. In this chapter, we provide several recommendations, and we briefly summarize the collected information that supports their implementation. Specifically, these recommendations draw from the previous research and interviews described in this report.

Better educate military service providers on how to provide gender-responsive support to male sexual assault victims.

Previous research regarding services available to sexual assault victims who are not in the military suggests that civilian service providers often focus on assisting female victims of sexual assault and can be ill-prepared to assist male victims (e.g., Donnelly and Kenyon, 1996). The experts we interviewed also raised concerns about the preparation of service providers and their support staff. Furthermore, many of the military service providers with whom we spoke noted that they had received little or no training on male sexual assault. Chaplains, in particular, indicated that individuals in their profession were not well informed about male sexual assault.

Overall, this suggests that military service providers who might interact with male sexual assault victims should receive specific training on how to assist these individuals. This training should inform service providers of the concerns and needs of male victims, including feelings of shame, feelings of self-blame, confusion regarding sexual identity, perceived loss of masculinity, and concerns over privacy.

To address common myths about male sexual assault, a training for service providers might be designed to describe and then dispel each myth; however, a growing body of evidence shows that this approach can *increase* the belief in myths (Schwarz, Newman, and Leach, 2016). To avoid this negative outcome, a better approach is to focus on the facts without repeating the myth. For example, dispelling the myth that "men can't be raped" could involve providing education about the number of servicemen who are sexually assaulted and reinforcing this new information by showing a video of a victim describing his experience. To dispel the myth that only gay men are raped, it could be important to include victim testimonial from a heterosexual man.

Training should also provide a grounding in the common experiences of male victims and the variance in male victim thoughts and actions following the assault. In addition, the training should include practice and role-play. This would give service providers some practice talking about the topic and the opportunity to receive feedback from a trainer about areas of strength and areas requiring additional practice. To the extent possible, training given to service providers on how to interact with male victims should be supported by previous research on effective techniques for assisting these victims (e.g., Vearnals and Campbell, 2001).

Promote male victim reporting by ensuring that reporting is safe and confidential.

An issue raised in previous research and during our interviews with experts and service providers is that the majority of male sexual assault victims are disinclined to report. In the military, this can include a disinclination to file restricted or unrestricted reports. These reports provide access to a variety of services for victims, but reporting is also related to a considerable risk of perceived professional reprisal, ostracism, and maltreatment (Severance, Debus, and Davis, 2017) and potential harm to the individual's career. In other words, victims make an individual calculus that weighs the benefits of reporting against the risks, and many decide that the risks are too considerable and the benefits too limited. Therefore, improving reporting rates will need to be a two-pronged approach. First, the reporting system must be improved until reassurances that reporting will not lead to retaliation or career harm are true. Second, victims should be encouraged to report. In the interim, victims should be provided with accurate information about the likely outcomes of their report and trusted to make the best, evidence-informed decision for themselves.

According to the service providers we interviewed, male victims are disinclined to report, in part, because of concerns about confidentiality. In fact, careful protection of confidentiality was highlighted as a primary need of victims. Providers indicated that male victims fear that their experience will be spread among providers and among commanders; that the assault or related help-seeking will be documented in a record following them through their career; and that even seemingly innocuous actions, such as entering a mental health clinic, will be observed by others and dispersed through their professional network. Not surprisingly, this fear of their confidentiality being broken represents a barrier to seeking services.

Despite considerable efforts to publicize the restricted reporting option and to educate all servicemembers about confidential reporting, it appears that, for many male victims, this messaging has not been heard or has not been believed. Specifically, servicemen might not receive sufficient information on confidential reporting options during the SAPR training they receive. Alternatively, they might receive the information but have difficulty recalling it. Another possibility is that men receive the information but distrust its veracity. Finally, if they are victimized, men may be disinclined to label their experience as a sexual assault because of feelings of shame, or they may genuinely believe that their experience was not a sexual assault because it was so different from the public perception of a typical sexual assault.

DoD may consider pursuing different options to promote reporting. One option is to address these potential issues in the training that servicemembers receive, which may include greater emphasis on DoD's intolerance for retaliation (DoD, 2016a). Additional options are to modify service provider intake forms and servicemember reporting options to better address the concerns of male sexual assault victims. For example, service provider intake forms may be modified to avoid reference to "sexual assault" and instead reference behaviorally specific experiences that would be categorized as sexual assault. This change to the language may assist with addressing the concerns that male victims appear to have regarding labeling their experience as a sexual assault. Furthermore, DoD might modify its Safe Helpline outreach materials to target military victims who may not label their experience as a sexual assault. Individuals could use this hotline to access a knowledgeable intake professional, and this professional could then direct the victims to others who could provide appropriate assistance and information. These modified outreach materials, however, should not replace existing outreach specific to a servicemember's experience, such as Safe Helpline's services to address sexual assault (Safe Helpline, undated-a).

Even in a system in which the confidentiality of those filing restricted reports is carefully guarded, it is also important to consider all the ways that victim confidentiality may be threatened and address these potential barriers. For example, even when the communication inside a SARC office is guarded, if the door to that office is in a public space where individuals may be seen entering or exiting, male victims could remain unwilling to use the service. In addition, the SARC office can provide assistance to men and women, but if it is seen as primarily catering to female needs and interests, male victims may be disinclined to go there.

Change outreach to better address the needs and concerns of male sexual assault victims.

Additional outreach campaigns that are targeted specifically to male sexual assault victims, rather than those that are gender-neutral or targeted to female victims, might better promote male victim reporting and help-seeking, as suggested by several experts and service providers. Being sexually assaulted can be interpreted by male victims as a threat to their masculinity. For example, providers commented that victims believe that they should have been able to stop the attack and that a "real man" would never have "allowed" it to happen. When the perpetrator is also a man, victims might be confused about the effect of the assault on their sexual orientation. Victims may turn these beliefs inward, or others who share the beliefs may express them to male victims. Thus, victims may experience self-blame and feel shamed by others. This shame may not only serve as a barrier to seeking services but also make it difficult for male victims to utilize mixed-gender services. Victims who feel shame, perceive stigma, and experience doubts about masculinity may find it challenging to absorb the information from a brochure or poster that primarily depicts women.

Nonetheless, service providers with whom we spoke commented that access to services was an important factor contributing to sexual assault victim reporting in the military. Therefore, additional or modified outreach campaigns can highlight the services available to male sexual assault victims who report. Given the difficulty that male victims have bearing the shame they associate with victimization and with help-seeking in general, it may be useful to highlight the easiest access points. Reaching out to a SARC or mental health care provider appears to be too high a hurdle for many male victims. To address this barrier, campaigns for men could emphasize services that do not require telephone conversations or in-person appointments. These access points include such services as text-based contact with the Safe Helpline and the DoD Safe HelpRoom, which is an anonymous online support board for victims that offers special sessions for men (Safe Helpline, undated-b).

Interviewees also indicated that obtaining justice and preventing others from being victimized are additional motivating factors for reporting. Outreach campaigns could highlight these factors. For example, highlighting that a victim who comes forward has the potential to stop other people from being assaulted may help men in particular regain a sense of healthy masculinity by reasserting a protector role. Messaging that reformulates help-seeking as a sign of strength and as a commitment to the mission may help male victims conceptualize help-seeking as being consistent with their masculinity rather than a threat to it. DoD has used these kinds of messages in programs to reduce stigma about mental health care and may be able to build on lessons learned when translating this expertise to sexual assault efforts (Acosta et al., 2014).

Finally, our interviewees noted that service providers should focus on providing assistance to victims, not pressuring individuals to report their assault through formal channels. Furthermore, campaigns to promote reporting among male sexual assault victims should not rely on military service providers to pressure victims to report.

When educating servicemembers on SAPR, use an engaging format that includes information on the characteristics of male sexual assault.

Servicemembers receive annual SAPR training. DoD Instruction 6495.02 requires that such training "shall incorporate adult learning theory, which includes interaction and group participation" (DoD, 2013). However, service providers with whom we spoke believed that the training often involves the use of didactic lectures that are complemented by PowerPoint presentations, which servicemembers do not find engaging. As required by DoD Instruction 6495.02, interactive discussion sessions with smaller groups of servicemembers and increased use of teaching techniques that promote active rather than passive learning may instill more knowledge and better promote information retention (Burke and Hutchins, 2007; Deslauriers, Schelew, and Wieman, 2011).

Based on the information provided by our interviewees, it is not clear whether additional SAPR training sessions that address only male sexual assault are needed. However, substantial portions of the training and education provided to servicemembers should specifically address male sexual assault. In particular, training and education should include information about the characteristics of male sexual assault among servicemembers, which may reference the occurrence of sexual assault during acts of hazing. To dispel common myths, education and training should focus on providing and reinforcing accurate information about the characteristics and experiences of victims as a way of reducing common misconceptions and stereotypes. Presentations from military male sexual assault victims, if possible, or presentations describing real stories of male sexual assault victims may maintain audience interest and knowledge retention.

Educate commanders on how to respond to male sexual assault and how to interact with male victims.

Our interviewees noted that, in order for male sexual assault victims to receive services (such as counseling or medical services), the victims may need support from their chain of command, and they need commanders to respect and help maintain victim privacy and confidentiality. Interviewees also indicated that victims are concerned about command and unit members retaliating against them, and some commanders may not believe that a male servicemember can be sexually assaulted. Some commanders might alienate male victims by, for example, failing to maintain confidentiality and privacy regarding the victim and assault or inquiring about the victim's sexual orientation.

To better address the needs of male sexual assault victims and their concerns regarding stigma, commanders should receive training that specifically addresses the sexual assault of male servicemembers. This training content should include common characteristics of male sexual assault in the military, needs and concerns of male sexual assault victims, and appropriate and inappropriate ways to interact with and assist these victims. This training should also emphasize the importance of maintaining victim privacy and confidentiality.

Consider development and evaluation of additional counseling services that address the mental health care needs of male sexual assault victims in the military.

Male sexual assault victims in the military may pursue many different support services. Service providers we interviewed indicated that they informed both male and female sexual assault victims of a variety of potential services available. Service providers also suggested that DoD could devote more resources to the development and implementation of counseling resources for male sexual assault victims in the military. In addition to assisting those assaulted while in the military, these resources may assist men who were victimized prior to joining the military.

Potential counseling services that DoD could consider developing, implementing, and evaluating include small, structured support groups with male sexual assault victims in the military. These victims may be particularly concerned about maintaining privacy and minimizing career effects. Furthermore, at any particular location, the number of reported male sexual assaults is limited. Therefore, DoD could consider increased use of online support groups or telephone-based support groups for these victims. Male sexual assault victims may also participate in support groups for others who have experienced different traumatic experiences in the military.

DoD may have difficulty assembling a large group of service providers with expertise in male sexual assault. For example, many service providers may assist only a small number of male sexual assault victims during their career. Following their service provider training on male sexual assault, discussed previously, service providers who see either a limited number of male sexual assault victims or no such victims might eventually have difficulty recalling appropriate treatment of and available services for these victims. Therefore, DoD may consider developing an established group of service providers who have experience with and are particularly knowledgeable about male sexual assault. These individuals could serve as moderators for online support groups and could be available to respond to the questions of service providers across various locations.

DoD might also consider expanding the available duty hours of installation clinics, such as mental health clinics. If counseling services are available for longer hours, male sexual assault victims may require less time away from their jobs to seek services, and this might, for example, reduce victim concerns regarding questions from peers and supervisors about why they require time away from work.

Support additional research that addresses the effects of training, outreach, and services addressing male sexual assault.

Very little research has examined the effects of training programs, counseling services, and outreach efforts that address male sexual assault. DoD should consider tracking service utilization among sexual assault victims who file an unrestricted report. By linking reports with medical and mental health records, researchers could determine whether victims are receiving appropriate follow-up care and investigate any differences in the quality of care that male and female victims receive following an assault. Given victims' desire for privacy and lack of confidence in the confidentiality associated with service-seeking, such a research project would have to be conducted under the highest standards for protection of human subjects data.

When implementing a new effort or modifying a current effort to better address male sexual assault in the armed forces, DoD should devote time and resources to evaluating the effectiveness of these efforts. For example, changes to service provider training should be evaluated to assess the effectiveness of these changes in preparing military service providers to support male sexual assault victims. Changes to service-member training and outreach should be evaluated to assess the impact of these new or modified efforts on servicemember knowledge, perceptions, and reporting behaviors relevant to male sexual assault. Assessments of counseling efforts can provide valuable information on the counseling format and structure preferred by male sexual assault victims and the effects of different forms of counseling on the psychological health of these individuals. Overall, systematic data collection and analysis can provide information about which elements are effective and which elements may need to be modified to better address the needs of servicemembers broadly and male sexual assault victims specifically.

Bibliography

Acosta, Joie D., Amariah Becker, Jennifer Cerully, Michael P. Fisher, Laurie T. Martin, Raffaele Vardavas, Mary Ellen Slaughter, and Terry Schell, *Mental Health Stigma in the Military*, Santa Monica, Calif.: RAND Corporation, RR-426-OSD, 2014. As of January 30, 2018: https://www.rand.org/pubs/research_reports/RR426.html

Anderson, Eric, Mark McCormack, and Harry Lee, "Male Team Sport Hazing Initiations in a Culture of Decreasing Homohysteria," *Journal of Adolescence Research*, Vol. 27, No. 4, 2012, pp. 427–448.

Anderson, Irina, and Alison Quinn, "Gender Differences in Medical Students' Attitudes Towards Male and Female Rape Victims," *Psychology, Health, and Medicine*, Vol. 14, No. 1, 2009, pp. 105–110.

Anderson, RaeAnn E., Shan P. Cahill, and Douglas L. Delahanty, "The Psychometric Properties of the Sexual Experiences Survey–Short Form Victimization (SES-SFV) and Characteristics of Sexual Victimization Experiences in College Men," *Psychology of Men and Masculinity*, September 2016.

Bachman, Ronet, *Measuring Rape and Sexual Assault: Successive Approximations to Consensus*, paper presented at National Academy of Sciences, Washington, D.C., June 6, 2012.

Bernard, H. Russell, and Gery W. Ryan, *Analyzing Qualitative Data: Systematic Approaches*, Washington D.C.: Sage, 2010.

Blosnich, John R., Melissa E. Dichter, Catherine Cerulli, Sonja V. Batten, and Robert M. Bossarte, "Disparities in Adverse Childhood Experiences Among Individuals with a History of Military Service," *JAMA Psychiatry*, Vol. 71, No. 9, 2014, pp. 1041–1048.

Breiding, Matthew J., Sharon G. Smith, Kathleen C. Basile, Mikel L. Walters, Jieru Chen, and Melissa T. Merrick, *Prevalence and Characteristics of Sexual Violence, Stalking, and Intimate Partner Violence Victimization—National Intimate Partner and Sexual Victimization Survey, United States, 2011*, Atlanta, Ga.: Centers for Disease Control and Prevention, 2014.

Bullock, Clayton M., and Mace Beckson, "Male Victims of Sexual Assault: Phenomenology, Psychology, and Physiology," *Journal of the American Academy of Psychiatry and the Law*, Vol. 39, No. 2, 2011, pp. 197–205.

Burke, Lisa A., and Holly M. Hutchins, "Training Transfer: An Integrative Literature Review," *Human Resource Development Review*, Vol. 6, No. 3, September 2007, pp. 263–296.

Campbell, Rebecca, "What Really Happened? A Validation Study of Rape Survivors' Help-Seeking Experiences with Legal and Medical Systems," *Violence and Victims*, Vol. 20, No. 1, 2005, pp. 55–68.

Castro, Carl Andrew, Sara Kintzle, Ashley C. Schuyler, Carrie L. Lucas, and Christopher H. Warner, "Sexual Assault in the Military," *Current Psychiatry Reports*, Vol. 17, No. 7, May 2015.

Chang, Bei-Hung, Katherine M. Skinner, Chunmei Zhou, and Lewis E. Kazis, "The Relationship Between Sexual Assault, Religiosity, and Mental Health Among Male Veterans," *International Journal of Psychiatry in Medicine*, Vol. 33, 2003, No. 3, pp. 223–239.

Chapleau, Kristine M., Debra L. Oswald, and Brenda L. Russell, "Male Rape Myths: The Role of Gender, Violence, and Sexism," *Journal of Interpersonal Violence*, Vol. 23, No. 5, 2008, pp. 600–615.

Choudhary, Ekta, Douglas Gunzler, Xin Tu, and Robert M. Bossarte, "Epidemiological Characteristics of Male Sexual Assault in a Criminological Database," *Journal of Interpersonal Violence*, Vol. 27, No. 3, 2012, pp. 523–546.

Cook, Mekeila C., Donald E. Morisky, John K. Williams, Chandra L. Ford, and Gilbert C. Gee, "Sexual Risk Behaviors and Substance Abuse Among Men Sexually Victimized by Women," *American Journal of Public Health*, Vol. 106, No. 7, 2016, pp. 1263–1269.

Cucciare, Michael A., Sharfun Ghaus, Kenneth R. Weingerdt, and Susan M. Frayen, "Sexual Assault and Substance Use in Male Victims Receiving a Brief Alcohol Intervention," *Journal of Studies on Alcohol and Drugs*, Vol. 72, No. 5, 2011, pp. 693–700.

Davies, Michelle, "Male Sexual Assault Victims: A Selective Review of the Literature and Implications for Support Services," *Aggression and Violent Behavior*, Vol. 7, No. 3, 2002, pp. 203–214.

Davies, Michelle, Jennifer Gilston, and Paul Rogers, "Examining the Relationship Between Male Rape Myth Acceptance, Female Rape Myth Acceptance, Victim Blame, Homophobia, Gender Roles, and Ambivalent Sexism," *Journal of Interpersonal Violence*, Vol. 27, No. 14, 2012, pp. 2807–2823.

Davies, Michelle, and Paul Rogers, "Perceptions of Male Victims in Depicted Sexual Assaults: A Review of the Literature," *Aggression and Violent Behavior*, Vol. 11, No. 4, 2006, pp. 367–377.

Davis, Lisa, Eric Falk, and Jeff Schneider, "Survey Methodology," in Lisa Davis, Amanda Grifka, Kristin Williams, and Margaret Coffey, eds., *2016 Workplace and Gender Relations Survey of Active Duty Members: Overview Report*, Alexandria, Va.: U.S. Department of Defense, Office of People Analytics, 2017, pp. 19–30. As of September 20, 2017:
http://www.sapr.mil/public/docs/reports/FY16_Annual/Annex_1_2016_WGRA_Report.pdf

Davis, Lisa, and Amanda Grifka, "Estimated Sexual Assault Prevalence Rates," in Lisa Davis, Amanda Grifka, Kristin Williams, and Margaret Coffey, eds., *2016 Workplace and Gender Relations Survey of Active Duty Members: Overview Report*, Alexandria, Va.: U.S. Department of Defense, Office of People Analytics, 2017a, pp. 31–50. As of September 20, 2017:
http://www.sapr.mil/public/docs/reports/FY16_Annual/Annex_1_2016_WGRA_Report.pdf

———, "One Situation of Sexual Assault with Biggest Effect," in Lisa Davis, Amanda Grifka, Kristin Williams, and Margaret Coffey, eds., *2016 Workplace and Gender Relations Survey of Active Duty Members: Overview Report*, Alexandria, Va.: U.S. Department of Defense, Office of People Analytics, 2017b, pp. 51–102. As of September 20, 2017:
http://www.sapr.mil/public/docs/reports/FY16_Annual/Annex_1_2016_WGRA_Report.pdf

Davis, Lisa, Amanda Grifka, Kristin Williams, and Margaret Coffey, eds., *2016 Workplace and Gender Relations Survey of Active Duty Members: Overview Report*, Alexandria, Va.: U.S. Department of Defense, Office of People Analytics, 2017. As of September 20, 2017:
http://www.sapr.mil/public/docs/reports/FY16_Annual/Annex_1_2016_WGRA_Report.pdf

Davis, Lisa, Ronald P. Vega, and Jeffrey McLeod, "Additional Descriptive Analyses and Future Directions," in Lisa Davis, Amanda Grifka, Kristin Williams, and Margaret Coffey, eds., *2016 Workplace and Gender Relations Survey of Active Duty Members: Overview Report*, Alexandria, Va.: U.S. Department of Defense, Office of People Analytics, 2017, pp. 355–367. As of September 20, 2017:
http://www.sapr.mil/public/docs/reports/FY16_Annual/Annex_1_2016_WGRA_Report.pdf

Dedoose, web application, Version 7.5.30, Los Angeles, Calif.: SocioCultural Research Consultants, LLC, 2017.

Department of the Army, *Fiscal Year 2016 Annual Report on Sexual Assault: U.S. Army*, Washington, D.C., 2013. As of September 27, 2017:
http://www.sapr.mil/public/docs/reports/FY16_Annual/Enclosure_1_Army_Annual_Report.pdf

Deslauriers, Louis, Ellen Schelew, and Carl Wieman, "Improved Learning in a Large-Enrollment Physics Class," *Science*, Vol. 332, No. 6031, May 2011, pp. 862–864.

DoD—*See* U.S. Department of Defense.

Doherty, Kathy, and Irina Anderson, "Making Sense of Male Rape: Constructions of Gender, Sexuality, and Experience of Rape Victims," *Journal of Community and Applied Social Psychology*, Vol. 14, No. 2, February 2004, pp. 85–103.

Donnelly, Denise A., and Stacy Kenyon, "'Honey, We Don't Do Men': Gender Stereotypes and the Provision of Services to Sexually Assaulted Males," *Journal of Interpersonal Violence*, Vol. 11, No. 3, 1996, pp. 441–448.

Elliott, Diana M., Doris S. Mok, and John Briere, "Adult Sexual Assault: Prevalence, Symptomatology, and Sex Differences in the General Population," *Journal of Traumatic Stress*, Vol. 17, No. 3, 2004, pp. 203–211.

Ernst, A. A., E. Green, M. T. Ferguson, S. J. Weiss, and W. M. Green, "The Utility of Anoscopy and Colposcopy in the Evaluation of Male Sexual Assault Victims," *Annals of Emergency Medicine*, Vol. 36, No. 5, 2000, pp. 432–437.

Farris, Coreen, Amy Street, Andrew R. Morral, Lisa Jaycox, and Dean Kilpatrick, "Measurement of Sexual Harassment and Sexual Assault," in Andrew R. Morral, Kristie L. Gore, and Terry L. Schell, eds., *Sexual Assault and Sexual Harassment in the U.S. Military: Volume 1. Design of the 2014 RAND Military Workplace Study*, Santa Monica, Calif.: RAND Corporation, RR-870/1-OSD, 2014, pp. 7–25. As of December 20, 2017:
https://www.rand.org/pubs/research_reports/RR870z1.html

Fisher, Bonnie S., "Measuring Rape Against Women: The Significance of Survey Questions," in Bonnie S. Fisher, ed., *Violence Against Women and Family Violence: Developments in Research, Practice, and Policy*, Washington, D.C.: U.S. Department of Justice, Office of Justice Programs, NCJ 199701, 2004, pp. I-4-1–I-4-16.

Fisher, Bonnie S., and Francis T. Cullen, "Measuring the Sexual Victimization of Women: Evolution, Current Controversies, and Future Research," in D. Duffee, ed., *Criminal Justice 2000*, Vol. 4, *Measurement and Analysis of Crime and Justice*, Washington, D.C.: U.S. Department of Justice, Office of Justice Programs, 2000, pp. 317–390.

Fuchs, Siegmund Fred, "Male Sexual Assault: Issues of Arousal and Consent," *Cleveland State Law Review*, Vol. 51, No. 1, 2004, pp. 93–121.

Franklin, Karen, "Enacting Masculinity: Antigay Violence and Group Rape as Participatory Theater," *Sexuality Research and Social Policy*, Vol. 1, No. 2, April 2004, pp. 26–40.

Frazier, Patricia A., "A Comparative Study of Male and Female Rape Victims Seen at a Hospital-Based Rape Crisis Program," *Journal of Interpersonal Violence*, Vol. 8, No. 1, March 1993, pp. 64–76.

Frazier, Patricia A., and Beth Haney, "Sexual Assault Cases in the Legal System: Police, Prosecutor, and Victim Perspectives," *Law and Human Behavior*, Vol. 20, No. 6, December 1996, pp. 607–628.

Ghosh-Dastidar, Bonnie, Terry L. Schell, Andrew R. Morral, and Marc N. Elliott, "The Efficacy of Sampling Weights for Correcting Nonresponse Bias," in Andrew R. Morral, Kristie L. Gore, and Terry L. Schell, eds., *Sexual Assault and Sexual Harassment in the U.S. Military: Volume 4. Investigations of Potential Bias in Estimates from the 2014 RAND Military Workplace Study*, Santa Monica, Calif.: RAND Corporation, RR-870/6-OSD, 2016, pp. 21–70. As of December 20, 2017: https://www.rand.org/pubs/research_reports/RR870z6.html

Gold, Sari D., Brian P. Marx, and Jennifer M. Lexington, "Gay Male Sexual Assault Survivors: The Relations Among Internalized Homophobia, Experiential Avoidance, and Psychological Symptom Severity," *Behaviour Research and Therapy*, Vol. 45, No. 3, 2007, pp. 549–562.

Guina, Jeffrey, Ramzi W. Nahhas, Kevin Kawalec, and Seth Farnsworth, "Are Gender Differences in DSM-5 PTSD Symptomology Explained by Sexual Trauma?" *Journal of Interpersonal Violence*, November 2016.

Hillman, Richard, Nigel O'Mara, David Tomlinson, and J. R. William Harris, "Adult Male Victims of Sexual Assault: An Underdiagnosed Condition," *International Journal of STD & AIDS*, Vol. 2, No. 1, 1991, pp. 22–24.

Hines, Denise A., "Predictors of Sexual Coercion Against Women and Men: A Multilevel, Multinational Study of University Students," *Archives of Sexual Behavior*, Vol. 36, No. 3, 2007, pp. 403–422.

Hodge, Samantha, and David Canter, "Victims and Perpetrators of Male Sexual Assault," *Journal of Interpersonal Violence*, Vol. 13, No. 2, 1998, pp. 222–239.

Holland, Kathryn J., Veronica Caridad Rabelo, and Lilia M. Cortina, "Sexual Assault Training in the Military: Evaluating Efforts to End the 'Invisible War,'" *American Journal of Community Psychology*, Vol. 54, No. 3–4, 2014, pp. 289–303.

Hoyt, Tim, Jennifer Klosterman Rielage, and Lauren F. Williams, "Military Sexual Trauma in Men: A Review of Reported Rates," *Journal of Trauma & Dissociation*, Vol. 12, No. 3, 2011, pp. 244–260.

———, "Military Sexual Trauma in Men: Exploring Treatment Principles," *Traumatology*, Vol. 18, No. 3, 2012, pp. 29–40.

Isely, Paul J., "Sexual Assault of Men: American Research Supports Studies from the UK," *Medicine, Science, and the Law*, Vol. 38, No. 1, 1998, pp. 74–80.

Isely, Paul J., and David Gehrenbeck-Shim, "Sexual Assault of Men in the Community," *Journal of Community Psychology*, Vol. 25, No. 2, March 1997, pp. 159–166.

Javaid, Aliraza, "Male Rape: The Unseen World of Male Rape," *Internet Journal of Criminology*, 2014, pp. 1–42.

———, "Male Rape Myths: Understanding and Explaining Social Attitudes Surrounding Male Rape," *Masculinities and Social Change*, Vol. 4, No. 3, 2015, pp. 270–294.

———, "Male Rape, Stereotypes, and Unmet Needs: Hindering Recovery, Perpetuating Silence," *Violence and Gender*, Vol. 3, No. 1, March 2016, pp. 7–13.

———, "Giving a Voice to Voiceless: Police Responses to Male Rape," *Policing*, Vol. 11, No. 2, June 2017, pp. 146–156.

Jaycox, Lisa H., Terry L. Schell, Coreen Farris, Amy Street, Dean Kilpatrick, Andrew R. Morral, and Terri Tanielian, "Questionnaire Development," in Andrew R. Morral, Kristie L. Gore, and Terry L. Schell, eds., *Sexual Assault and Sexual Harassment in the U.S. Military: Volume 1. Design of the 2014 RAND Military Workplace Study*, Santa Monica, Calif.: RAND Corporation, RR-870/1-OSD, 2014, pp. 37–56. As of December 20, 2017: https://www.rand.org/pubs/research_reports/RR870z1.html

Jaycox, Lisa H., Terry L. Schell, Andrew R. Morral, Amy Street, Coreen Farris, Dean Kilpatrick, and Terri Tanielian, "Sexual Assault Findings: Active Component," in Andrew R. Morral, Kristie L. Gore, and Terry L. Schell, eds., *Sexual Assault and Sexual Harassment in the U.S. Military: Volume 2. Estimates for Department of Defense Servicemembers from the 2014 RAND Military Workplace Study*, Santa Monica, Calif.: RAND Corporation, RR-870/2-1-OSD, 2015, pp. 9–30. As of December 20, 2017:
https://www.rand.org/pubs/research_reports/RR870z2-1.html

Kassing, Leslee R., Denise Beesley, and Lisa L. Frey, "Gender Role Conflict, Homophobia, Age, and Education as Predictors of Male Rape Myth Acceptance," *Journal of Mental Health Counseling*, Vol. 27, No. 4, 2005, pp. 311–328.

Kassing, Leslee R., and Loreto R. Prieto, "The Rape Myth and Blame-Based Beliefs of Counselors in Training Toward Male Victims of Rape," *Journal of Counseling and Development*, Vol. 81, No. 4, 2003, pp. 455–461.

Keller, Kirsten M., Miriam Matthews, Kimberly Curry Hall, William Marcellino, Jacqueline A. Mauro, and Nelson Lim, *Hazing in the U.S. Armed Forces: Recommendations for Hazing Prevention Policy and Practice*, Santa Monica, Calif.: RAND Corporation, RR-941-OSD, 2015. As of December 20, 2017:
https://www.rand.org/pubs/research_reports/RR941.html

Kilpatrick, Dean G., "What Is Violence Against Women? Defining and Measuring the Problem," *Journal of Interpersonal Violence*, Vol. 19, No. 11, 2004, pp. 1209–1234.

Kimerling, Rachel, Amy E. Street, Joanne Pavao, Mark W. Smith, Ruth C. Cronkite, Tyson H. Holmes, and Susan M. Frayne, "Military-Related Sexual Trauma Among Veterans Health Administration Patients Returning from Iraq and Afghanistan," *American Journal of Public Health*, Vol. 100, No. 8, August 2010, pp. 1409–1412.

King, Michael, and Earnest Woollett, "Sexually Assaulted Males: 115 Men Consulting a Counseling Service," *Archives of Sexual Behavior*, Vol. 26, No. 6, December 1997, pp. 579–588.

Kirby, Sandra L., and Glen Wintrup, "Running the Gauntlet: An Examination of Initiation/Hazing and Sexual Abuse in Sport," *Journal of Sexual Aggression*, Vol. 8, 2002, pp. 49–68.

Lamothe, Dan, "Male on Male Sexual Assault in the Military: Overlooked and Hard to Fix, Investigation Finds," *Washington Post*, March 20, 2015.

Langenderfer-Magruder, Lisa, N. Eugene Walls, Shanna K. Kattari, Darren L. Whitfield, and Daniel Ramos, "Sexual Victimization and Subsequent Police Reporting by Gender Identity Among Lesbian, Gay, Bisexual, Transgender, and Queer Adults," *Violence and Victims*, Vol. 31, No. 2, 2016, pp. 320–331.

Lapp, Kathleen G., Hayden B. Bosworth, Jennifer L. Strauss, Karen M. Stechuchak, Ron D. Horner, Patrick S. Calhoun, Keith G. Meador, Steven Lipper, and Marian I. Butterfield, "Lifetime Sexual and Physical Victimization Among Male Veterans with Combat-Related Post-Traumatic Stress Disorder," *Military Medicine*, Vol. 170, September 2005, pp. 787–790.

Light, David, and Elizabeth Monk-Turner, "Circumstances Surrounding Male Sexual Assault and Rape: Findings from the National Violence Against Women Survey," *Journal of Interpersonal Violence*, Vol. 24, No. 11, 2009, pp. 1849–1858.

Maguen, Shira, Beth Cohen, Li Ren, Jeane Bosch, Rachel Kimerling, and Karen Seal, "Gender Differences in Military Sexual Trauma and Mental Health Diagnoses Among Iraq and Afghanistan Veterans with Posttraumatic Stress Disorder," *Women's Health Issues*, Vol. 22, No. 1, 2012, pp. e61–e66.

Management of Major Depressive Disorder Working Group, *VA/DoD Clinical Practice Guideline for the Management of Major Depressive Disorder*, Washington, D.C.: U.S. Department of Veterans Affairs and U.S. Department of Defense, Version 3.0, April 2016. As of January 27, 2017: https://www.healthquality.va.gov/guidelines/MH/mdd/VADoDMDDCPGFINAL82916.pdf

Management of Post-Traumatic Stress Working Group, *VA/DoD Clinical Practice Guideline for Management of Post-Traumatic Stress*, Washington, D.C.: U.S. Department of Veterans Affairs and U.S. Department of Defense, Version 2.0, October 2010. As of January 27, 2017: http://www.healthquality.va.gov/PTSD-full-2010c.pdf

Martin, Lee, Leora Rosen, and Doris Briley Durand, "Prevalence and Timing of Sexual Assaults in a Sample of Male and Female U.S. Army Soldiers," *Military Medicine*, Vol. 163, No. 4, April 1998, pp. 213–216.

Martin, Lee, Leora Rosen, Doris B. Durand, Kathryn H. Knudson, and Robert H. Stretch, "Psychological and Physical Health Effects of Sexual Assaults and Nonsexual Traumas Among Male and Female United States Army Soldiers," *Behavioral Medicine*, Vol. 26, No. 1, 2000, pp. 23–33.

Masho, Saba W., and Anika Alvanzo, "Help-Seeking Behaviors of Men Sexual Assault Survivors," *American Journal of Men's Health*, Vol. 4, No. 3, September 2009, pp. 237–242.

McLean, Iain, "The Male Victim of Sexual Assault," *Best Practice & Research Clinical Obstetrics and Gynecology*, Vol. 27, No. 1, 2013, pp. 39–46.

McMahon, Pamela M., "The Public Health Approach to the Prevention of Sexual Assault," *Sexual Abuse: A Journal of Research and Treatment*, Vol. 12, No. 1, 2000, pp. 27–36.

Mezey, Gillian, and Michael King, "Male Victims of Sexual Assault," *Medicine, Science, and the Law*, Vol. 27, No. 2, April 1987, pp. 122–124.

Millegan, Jeffrey, Lawrence Wang, Cynthia A. LeardMann, Derek Miletich, and Amy E. Street, "Sexual Trauma and Adverse Health and Occupational Outcomes Among Men Serving in the U.S. Military," *Journal of Traumatic Stress*, Vol. 29, No. 2, April 2016, pp. 132–140.

Mitchell, Damon, Richard Hirschman, and Gordon C. Nagayama Hall, "Attributions of Victim Responsibility, Pleasure, and Trauma in Male Rapes," *Journal of Sex Research*, Vol. 36, No. 4, 1999, pp. 369–373.

Modi, Danbaba Enoch, and Ojo Matthias Olufemi Dada, "Myths and Effects of Rape on Male Victims," *American Journal of Psychology and Cognitive Science*, Vol. 1, No. 1, 2015, pp. 1–5.

Mondragon, Sasha A., David Wang, Loniquw Pritchett, David P. Graham, M. Leili Plasencia, and Ellen J. Teng, "The Influence of Military Sexual Trauma on Returning OEF/OIF Male Veterans," *Psychological Services*, Vol. 12, No. 4, 2015, pp. 402–411.

Monk-Turner, Elizabeth, and David Light, "Male Sexual Assault and Rape: Who Seeks Counseling?" *Sexual Abuse: A Journal of Research and Treatment*, Vol. 22, No. 3, August 2010, pp. 255–265.

Morral, Andrew R., Kristie L. Gore, and Terry L. Schell, eds., *Sexual Assault and Sexual Harassment in the U.S. Military: Volume 1. Design of the 2014 RAND Military Workplace Study*, Santa Monica, Calif.: RAND Corporation, RR-870/1-OSD, 2014. As of December 20, 2017: https://www.rand.org/pubs/research_reports/RR870z1.html

———, eds., *Sexual Assault and Sexual Harassment in the U.S. Military: Annex to Volume 2. Tabular Results from the 2014 RAND Military Workplace Study for Department of Defense Servicemembers*, Santa Monica, Calif.: RAND Corporation, 2015a. As of December 20, 2017: https://www.rand.org/pubs/research_reports/RR870z3.html

————, eds., *Sexual Assault and Sexual Harassment in the U.S. Military: Volume 2. Estimates for Department of Defense Servicemembers from the 2014 RAND Military Workplace Study*, Santa Monica, Calif.: RAND Corporation, RR-870/2-1-OSD, 2015b. As of December 20, 2017: https://www.rand.org/pubs/research_reports/RR870z2-1.html

Morral, Andrew R., Terry L. Schell, Matthew Cefalu, Jessica Hwang, and Andrew Gelman, *Sexual Assault and Sexual Harassment in the U.S. Military: Volume 5. Estimates for Installation- and Command-Level Risk of Sexual Assault and Sexual Harassment from the 2014 RAND Military Workplace Study*, Santa Monica, Calif.: RAND Corporation, RR-870/7-OSD, forthcoming.

Morris, E. Ellen, Julia C. Smith, Sharjeel Yonus Farooqui, and Alina M. Suris, "Unseen Battles: The Recognition, Assessment, and Treatment Issues of Men with Military Sexual Trauma (MST)," *Trauma, Violence, and Abuse*, Vol. 15, No. 2, 2014, pp. 94–101.

Muehlenhard, Charlene M., and Stephen W. Cook, "Men's Self-Reports of Unwanted Sexual Activity," *Journal of Sex Research*, Vol. 24, 1988, pp. 58–72.

Mullen, Kacy, Ryan Holliday, Ellen Morris, Annia Raja, and Alina Suris, "Cognitive Processing Therapy for Male Veterans with Military Sexual Trauma-Related Posttraumatic Stress Disorder," *Journal of Anxiety Disorders*, Vol. 28, Vol. 8, December 2014, pp. 761–764.

Murdoch, Maureen, Melissa A. Polusny, James Hodges, and Nancy O'Brien, "Prevalence of In-Service and Post-Service Sexual Assault Among Combat and Noncombat Veterans Applying for Department of Veterans Affairs Posttraumatic Stress Disorder Disability Benefits," *Military Medicine*, Vol. 169, No. 5, May 2004, pp. 392–395.

Murdoch, Maureen, Melissa A. Polusny, Amy Street, Siamak Noorbaloochi, Alisha B. Simon, Ann Bangerter, Joseph Grill, and Emily Voller, "Sexual Assault During the Time of Gulf War I: A Cross-Sectional Survey of U.S. Service Men Who Later Applied for Department of Veterans Affairs PTSD Disability Benefits," *Military Medicine*, Vol. 179, Vol. 3, March 2014, pp. 285–293.

Murdoch, Maureen, John Barron Pryor, Melissa Anderson Polusny, and Gary Dean Gackstetter, "Functioning and Psychiatric Symptoms Among Military Men and Women Exposed to Sexual Stressors," *Military Medicine*, Vol. 172, Vol. 7, July 2007, pp. 718–725.

National Research Council, "Estimating the Incidence of Rape and Sexual Assault," in Candace Kruttschnitt, William D. Kalsbeek, and Carol C. House, eds., *Panel on Measuring Rape and Sexual Assault in Bureau of Justice Household Surveys*, Washington, D.C.: National Academies Press, 2014.

O'Brien, Carol, Jessica Keith, and Lisa Shoemaker, "Don't Tell: Military Culture and Male Rape," *Psychological Services*, Vol. 12, No. 4, 2015, pp. 357–365.

Patton, Michael Quinn, *Qualitative Research and Evaluation Methods*, 4th ed., Washington D.C.: Sage, 2015.

Pesola, Gene R., Richard E. Westfal, and Carol A. Kuffner, "Emergency Department Characteristics of Male Sexual Assault," *Academic Emergency Medicine*, Vol. 6, No. 8, 1999, pp. 792–798.

Peterson, Zoe, and Charlene L. Muehlenhard, "Was It Rape? The Function of Women's Rape Myth Acceptance and Definition of Sex in Labeling Their Own Experiences," *Sex Roles*, Vol. 51, No. 3–4, 2004, pp. 129–144.

Peterson, Zoe, Emily K. Voller, Melissa A. Polusny, and Maureen Murdoch, "Prevalence and Consequences of Adult Sexual Assault of Men: Review of Empirical Findings and State of the Literature," *Clinical Psychology Review*, Vol. 31, No. 1, 2011, pp. 1–24.

Pino, Nathan W., and Robert F. Meier, "Gender Differences in Rape Reporting," *Sex Roles*, Vol. 40, No. 11–12, June 1999, pp. 979–990.

Polusny, Melissa A., and Maureen Murdoch, "Sexual Assault Among Male Veterans," *Psychiatric Times*, Vol. 22, No. 4, April 2005.

Public Law 114-92, National Defense Authorization Act for Fiscal Year 2016, November 25, 2015.

Rape, Abuse, and Incest National Network, "Key Terms and Phrases," webpage, 2016. As of May 30, 2017:
https://www.rainn.org/articles/key-terms-and-phrases

Rentoul, Lynette, and N. Appleboom, "Understanding the Psychological Impact of Rape and Serious Sexual Assault of Men: A Literature Review," *Journal of Psychiatric and Mental Health Nursing*, Vol. 4, No. 4, August 1997, pp. 267–274.

Riggs, N., D. Houry, G. Long, V. Markovchick, and K. M. Feldhaus, "Analysis of 1,076 Cases of Sexual Assault," *Annals of Emergency Medicine*, Vol. 35, No. 4, April 2000, pp. 358–360.

Romano, Elisa, and Rayleen De Luca, "Male Sexual Abuse: A Review of Effects, Abuse Characteristics, and Links with Later Psychological Functioning," *Aggression and Violent Behavior*, Vol. 6, No. 1, 2001, pp. 55–78.

Rosenstein, Judith E., "Military Sexual Assault Prevention and Male Rape Myth Acceptance," *Military Behavioral Health*, Vol. 3, No. 4, May 2015, pp. 207–211.

Sable, Marjorie, Fran Danis, Denise L. Mauzy, and Sarah K. Gallagher, "Barriers to Reporting Sexual Assault for Women and Men," *Journal of American College Health*, Vol. 55, No. 3, 2006, pp. 157–162.

Sadler, Anne G., Brenda M. Booth, Brian L. Cook, James C. Torner, and Bradley N. Doebbeling, "The Military Environment: Risk Factors for Women's Non-Fatal Assault," *Journal of Occupational and Environmental Medicine*, Vol. 43, No. 4, April 2001, pp. 325–334.

Safe Helpline, homepage, undated-a. As of June 27, 2017:
https://www.safehelpline.org/

———, "About Safe HelpRoom," webpage, undated-b. As of January 22, 2018:
https://www.safehelpline.org/about-safe-helproom

Scarce, Michael, "Same-Sex Rape of Male College Students," *Journal of American College Health*, Vol. 45, No. 4, 1997, pp. 171–173.

Schell, Terry L., Coreen Farris, Lisa H. Jaycox, Dean G. Kilpatrick, and Amy E. Street, "Correspondence Between the RMWS Measure of Sexual Assault and Title 10 USC § 920 (UCMJ Article 120)," in Andrew R. Morral, Kristie L. Gore, and Terry L. Schell, eds., *Sexual Assault and Sexual Harassment in the U.S. Military: Volume 1. Design of the 2014 RAND Military Workplace Study*, Santa Monica, Calif.: RAND Corporation, RR-870/1-OSD, 2014, pp. 81–90. As of December 20, 2017:
https://www.rand.org/pubs/research_reports/RR870z1.html

Schry, Amie R., Rachel Hibbard, H. Ryan Wagner, Jessica A. Turchik, Nathan A. Kimbrel, Madrianne Wong, Eric E. Elbogen, Jennifer L. Strauss, Veterans Affairs Mid-Atlantic Mental Illness Research, Education and Clinical Center Workgroup, and Mira Brancu, "Functional Correlates of Military Sexual Assault in Male Victims," *Psychological Services*, Vol. 12, No. 4, November 2015, pp. 384–393.

Schwarz, Norbert, Eryn Newman, and William Leach, "Making the Truth Stick and the Myths Fade: Lessons from Cognitive Psychology," *Behavioral Science and Policy*, Vol. 2, No. 1, 2016, pp. 85–95.

Severance, Laura, Jason Debus, and Lisa Davis, "An Analysis of Men Who Indicate Experiencing Sexual Assault," in Lisa Davis, Amanda Grifka, Kristin Williams, and Margaret Coffey, eds., *2016 Workplace and Gender Relations Survey of Active Duty Members: Overview Report*, Alexandria, Va.: U.S. Department of Defense, Office of People Analytics, 2017, pp. 313–344. As of September 20, 2017:
http://www.sapr.mil/public/docs/reports/FY16_Annual/Annex_1_2016_WGRA_Report.pdf

Sivakumaran, Sandesh, "Male/Male Rape and the 'Taint' of Homosexuality," *Human Rights Quarterly*, Vol. 27, No. 4, 2005, pp. 1274–1306.

Sleath, Emma, and Ray Bull, "Male Rape Victim and Perpetrator Blaming," *Journal of Interpersonal Violence*, Vol. 25, No. 6, 2010, pp. 969–988.

Smith, Philip H., Marc N. Potenza, Carolyn M. Mazure, Sherry A. McKee, Crystal L. Park, and Rani A. Hoff, "Compulsive Sexual Behavior Among Male Military Veterans: Prevalence and Associated Clinical Factors," *Journal of Behavioral Addictions*, Vol. 3, No. 4, December 2014, pp. 214–222.

Smith, Ronald E., Charles J. Pine, and Mark E. Hawley, "Social Cognitions About Adult Male Victims of Female Sexual Assault," *Journal of Sex Research*, Vol. 24, No. 1, January 1988, pp. 101–112.

Stemple, Lara, and Ilan H. Meyer, "The Sexual Victimization of Men in America: New Data Challenge Old Assumptions," *American Journal of Public Health*, Vol. 104, No. 6, 2014, pp. e19–e26.

Stermac, Lana, Giannetta del Bove, and Mary Addison, "Stranger and Acquaintance Sexual Assault of Adult Males," *Journal of Interpersonal Violence*, Vol. 19, No. 8, August 2004, pp. 901–915.

Stotzer, Rebecca, "Violence Against Transgender People: A Review of United States Data," *Aggression and Violent Behavior*, Vol. 14, No. 3, 2009, pp. 170–179.

Struckman-Johnson, Cindy, "Forced Sex on Dates: It Happens to Men Too," *Journal of Sex Research*, Vol. 24, 1988, pp. 234–241.

Tewksbury, Richard, "Effects of Sexual Assault on Men: Physical, Mental, and Sexual Consequences," *International Journal of Men's Health*, Vol. 6, No. 1, Spring 2007, pp. 22–35.

Tiet, Quyen Q., John W. Finney, and Rudolf H. Moos, "Recent Sexual Abuse, Physical Abuse, and Suicide Attempts Among Male Veterans Seeking Psychiatric Treatment," *Psychiatric Services*, Vol. 57, No. 1, 2006, pp. 107–113.

Tiet, Quyen Q., Yani E. Leyva, Kathy Blau, Jessica A. Turchik, and Craig S. Rosen, "Military Sexual Assault, Gender, and PTSD Treatment Outcomes of U.S. Veterans," *Journal of Traumatic Stress*, Vol. 28, No. 2, April 2015, pp. 92–101.

Tomlinson, D. R., and J. Harrison, "The Management of Adult Male Victims of Sexual Assault in the GUM Clinic: A Practical Guide," *International Journal of STD & AIDS*, Vol. 9, No. 12, December 1998, pp. 720–725.

Tracy, Carol E., Terry L. Fromson, Jennifer G. Long, and Charlene Whitman, *Rape and Sexual Assault in the Legal System*, Washington, D.C.: U.S. Department of Justice, Bureau of Justice Statistics, 2012.

Turchik, Jessica A., and Katie M. Edwards, "Myths About Male Rape: A Literature Review," *Psychology of Men & Masculinity*, Vol. 13, No. 2, 2012, pp. 211–226.

Turchik, Jessica A., Caitlin McLean, Samantha Rafie, Tim Hoyt, Craig S. Rosen, and Rachel Kimerling, "Perceived Barriers to Care and Provider Gender Preferences Among Veteran Men Who Have Experienced Military Sexual Trauma: A Qualitative Analysis," *Psychological Services*, Vol. 10, No. 2, May 2013, pp. 213–222.

Turchik, Jessica A., Joanne Pavao, Jenny Hyun, Hanna Mark, and Rachel Kimerling, "Utilization and Intensity of Outpatient Care Related to Military Sexual Trauma for Veterans from Afghanistan and Iraq," *Journal of Behavioral Health Services & Research*, Vol. 39, No. 3, July 2012, pp. 220–233.

Turchik, Jessica A., Joanne Pavao, Deborah Nazarian, Samina Iqbal, Caitlin McLean, and Rachel Kimerling, "Sexually Transmitted Infections and Sexual Dysfunctions Among Newly Returned Veterans With and Without Military Sexual Trauma," *International Journal of Sexual Health*, Vol. 24, No. 1, 2012, pp. 45–59.

Turchik, Jessica A., Samantha Rafie, Craig S. Rosen, and Rachel Kimerling, "Preferences for Gender-Targeted Health Information: A Study of Male Veterans Who Have Experienced Military Sexual Trauma," *American Journal of Men's Health*, Vol. 8, No. 3, May 2014, pp. 240–248.

Turchik, Jessica A., and Susan M. Wilson, "Sexual Assault in the U.S. Military: A Review of the Literature and Recommendations for the Future," *Aggression and Violent Behavior*, Vol. 15, No. 4, 2010, pp. 267–277.

Ullman, Sarah E., and Henrietta H. Filipas, "Predictors of PTSD Symptom Severity and Social Reactions in Sexual Assault Victims," *Journal of Traumatic Stress*, Vol. 14, No. 2, April 2001, pp. 369-389.

United States Code, Title 10, Section 920, Rape and Sexual Assault Generally.

U.S. Department of Defense, *Sexual Assault Prevention and Response (SAPR) Program*, Washington, D.C., DoD Directive 6495.01, January 23, 2012. As of January 17, 2018:
http://www.vi.ngb.army.mil/html/sapr/docs/DoD%20Directive%206495.01.pdf

———, *Sexual Assault Prevention and Response (SAPR) Program Procedures*, Washington, D.C., DoD Instruction 6495.02, March 28, 2013. As of September 25, 2017:
http://www.sapr.mil/public/docs/directives/649502p.pdf

———, *DoD Retaliation Prevention and Response Strategy: Regarding Sexual Assault and Harassment Reports*, Washington, D.C., April 2016a. As of July 26, 2017:
http://sapr.mil/public/docs/reports/Retaliation/DoD_Retaliation_Strategy.pdf

———, *Plan to Prevent and Respond to Sexual Assault of Military Men*, Washington, D.C., October 2016b. As of September 25, 2017:
http://sapr.mil/public/docs/prevention/
DoD-Plan-to-Prevent-and-Respond-to-Sexual-Assault-of-Military-Men_Approved.pdf

Vearnals, Simon, and Tomas Campbell, "Male Victims of Male Sexual Assault: A Review of Psychological Consequences and Treatment," *Sexual and Relationship Therapy*, Vol. 16, No. 3, 2001, pp. 279–286.

Villejoubert, Gaëlle, and David R. Mandel, "The Inverse Fallacy: An Account of Deviations from Bayes's Theorem and the Additivity Principle," *Memory and Cognition*, Vol. 30, No. 2, 2002, pp. 171–178.

Voelkel, Emily, Nicole D. Pukay-Martin, Kristin H. Walter, and Kathleen M. Chard, "Effectiveness of Cognitive Processing Therapy for Male and Female U.S. Veterans With and Without Military Sexual Trauma," *Journal of Traumatic Stress*, Vol. 28, No. 3, June 2015, pp. 174–182.

Voller, Emily, Melissa A. Polusny, Siamak Noorbaloochi, Amy Street, Joseph Grill, and Maureen Murdoch, "Self-Efficacy, Male Rape Myth Acceptance, and Devaluation of Emotions in Sexual Trauma Sequelae: Findings from a Sample of Male Veterans," *Psychological Services*, Vol. 12, No. 4, November 2015, pp. 420–427.

Walker, Jayne, John Archer, and Michelle Davies, "Effects of Rape on Men: A Descriptive Analysis," *Archives of Sexual Behavior*, Vol. 34, No. 1, February 2005, pp. 69–80.

Wall, Barry W., "Commentary: Causes and Consequences of Male Adult Sexual Assault," *Journal of the American Academy of Psychiatry and the Law*, Vol. 39, No. 2, 2011, pp. 206–208.

Washington, Patricia A., "Second Assault of Male Survivors of Sexual Violence," *Journal of Interpersonal Violence*, Vol. 14, No. 7, 1999, pp. 713–730.

Weiss, Karen G., "Male Sexual Victimization: Examining Men's Experiences of Rape and Sexual Assault," *Men and Masculinities*, Vol. 12, No. 3, 2010, pp. 275–298.

Williams, D. J., Emily Prior, and Jenna Wegner, "Resolving Social Problems Associated with Sexuality: Can a Sex-Positive Approach Help?" *Social Work*, Vol. 58, No. 3, July 2013, pp. 273–276.

WorldCat, homepage, Online Computer Library Center, undated. As of April 26, 2017: http://www.oclc.org/en/worldcat-org.html

Zweig, Janine M., Bonnie L. Barber, and Jacquelynne Eccles, "Sexual Coercion and Well-Being in Young Adulthood: Comparisons by Gender and College Status," *Journal of Interpersonal Violence*, Vol. 12, No. 2, 1997, pp. 291–308.